Access to History

General Editor: Keith Randell

The Ottoman Empire
1450–1700

Access to History

General Editor: Keith Randell

The Ottoman Empire 1450–1700

Andrina Stiles

Hodder & Stoughton

A MEMBER OF THE HODDER HEADLINE GROUP

The cover illustration is a portrait of Suleiman the Magnificent painted by Nigari (Haydar Reis) in about 1560 Courtesy Topkapi Saray Museum.

Some other titles in the series:

Spain, Rise and Decline 1474–1643　　　　　　ISBN 0 340 51807 3
Jill Kilsby

Sweden and the Baltic 1523–1721　　　　　　ISBN 0 340 54644 1
Andrina Stiles

From Revolt to Independence:　　　　　　ISBN 0 340 51803 0
The Netherlands 1550–1650
Martyn Rady

Charles V: Ruler, Dynast and Defender　　　　　ISBN 0 340 53558 X
of the Faith 1500–58
Stewart MacDonald

Europe and the Enlightened Despots　　　　　ISBN 0 340 53559 8
Walter Oppenheim

British Library Cataloguing in Publication Data
Stiles, Andrina
    The Ottoman Empire 1450–1700. — (Access to history).
    1. Ottoman Empire, History
    I. Title   II. Series
    956

ISBN 0–340–56999–9

First published in the Access to A-Level History series 1989
This edition published 1991

Impression number 10　9　8　7　6　5　4　3
Year　　　　　　　1998　1997　1996　1995

Typeset by Wearset, Boldon, Tyne and Wear.
Printed in Great Britain for Hodder and Stoughton Educational, a division of Hodder Headline Plc, 338 Euston Road, London NW1 3BH by Page Bros, Norwich.

Contents

Preface

To the general reader

Although the *Access to History* series has been designed with the needs of students studying the subject at higher examination levels very much in mind, it also has a great deal to offer the general reader. The main body of the text (i.e. ignoring the Study Guides at the ends of chapters) forms a readable and yet stimulating survey of a coherent topic as studied by historians. However, each author's aim has not merely been to provide a clear explanation of what happened in the past (to interest and inform): it has also been assumed that most readers wish to be stimulated into thinking further about the topic and to form opinions of their own about the significance of the events that are described and discussed (to be challenged). Thus, although no prior knowledge of the topic is expected on the reader's part, she or he is treated as an intelligent and thinking person throughout. The author tends to share ideas and possibilities with the reader, rather than passing on numbers of so-called 'historical truths'.

To the student reader

There are many ways in which the series can be used by students studying History at a higher level. It will, therefore, be worthwhile thinking about your own study strategy before you start your work on this book. Obviously, your strategy will vary depending on the aim you have in mind, and the time for study that is available to you.

If, for example, you want to acquire a general overview of the topic in the shortest possible time, the following approach will probably be the most effective:

1. Read Chapter 1 and think about its contents.
2. Read the 'Making notes' section at the end of Chapter 2 and decide whether it is necessary for you to read this chapter.
3. If it is, read the chapter, stopping at each heading or * to note down the main points that have been made.
4. Repeat stage 2 (and stage 3 where appropriate) for all the other chapters.

If, however, your aim is to gain a thorough grasp of the topic, taking however much time is necessary to do so, you may benefit from carrying out the same procedure with each chapter, as follows:

1. Read the chapter as fast as you can, and preferably at one sitting.
2. Study the flow diagram at the end of the chapter, ensuring that you understand the general 'shape' of what you have just read.
3. Read the 'Making notes' section (and the 'Answering essay

questions' section, if there is one) and decide what further work you need to do on the chapter. In particularly important sections of the book, this will involve reading the chapter a second time and stopping at each heading and * to think about (and to write a summary of) what you have just read.

4. Attempt the 'Source-based questions' section. It will sometimes be sufficient to think through your answers, but additional understanding will often be gained by forcing yourself to write them down.

When you have finished the main chapters of the book, study the 'Further Reading' section and decide what additional reading (if any) you will do on the topic.

This book has been designed to help make your studies both enjoyable and successful. If you can think of ways in which this could have been done more effectively, please write to tell me. In the meantime, I hope that you will gain greatly from your study of History.

Keith Randell

CHAPTER 1

The Ottoman Empire in the Mid-fifteenth Century

1 The Fall of Constantinople

On the 29 May 1453 the city of Constantinople fell to the Ottomans (more commonly referred to in the West at the time as the Turks – see page 9). Its fate had long been inevitable but it still came as a shock to Christian Europe.

The city, named in honour of the Emperor Constantine over a thousand years earlier, had been founded by the Romans on the old Greek city of Byzantium. It stood on a triangular promontory, surrounded by water on two sides, with one of the most beautiful, natural harbours in the world, the Golden Horn. Poised between Europe and Asia, it was the capital of what remained of the Eastern Roman Empire, or, as it was still called, the Byzantine Empire. The city was much decayed by the middle of the fifteenth century. What had been a population of more than a million in the twelfth century had shrunk to less than a hundred thousand. The suburbs, once rich and filled with magnificent villas, monasteries and public buildings had been reduced to mere villages of a few houses grouped around an ancient and crumbling church. The imperial palace was largely uninhabitable, and only at the university did life go on much as it always had, with the scholars continuing to dazzle the world with their brilliance.

In January 1453 the new young Ottoman Sultan, Mehmed II, assembled his ministers and told them that the Ottoman Empire would never be secure until Constantinople was in Ottoman hands. This was not strictly true. There was no strategic necessity for its capture (however politically desirable it might be), for the Byzantine emperors were already in effect Ottoman vassals, and presented no threat. The overwhelming reason for taking the city was one of prestige. Earlier attempts by his predecessors to do so had failed, for the massive triple wall and deep fosse (dry ditch) sixty feet wide had resisted prolonged sieges. Both sides began to make preparations. The Sultan gathered a large fleet of galleys and other smaller ships. There were probably about 130 vessels altogether. They made their way through the Dardanelles and anchored in the Bosphorus (see diagram 1) at the end of March, while the Ottoman army, probably about 150000 strong, gathered in Thrace, the Ottoman-controlled lands to the west of the city. It was a well-disciplined and well-equipped army, and had a number of the newfangled cannon, which fired stone balls weighing more than half a

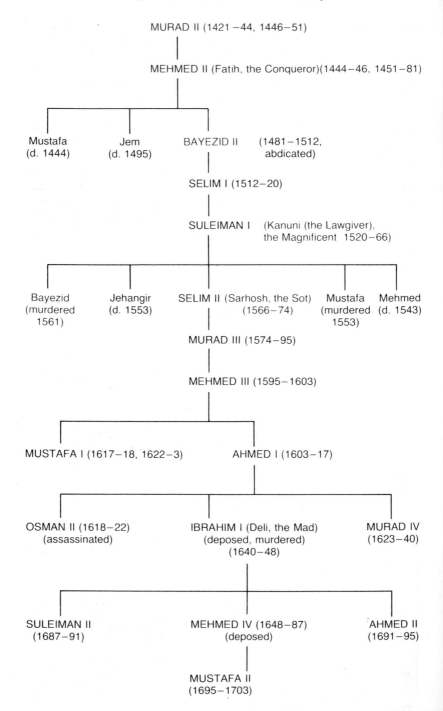

ton. The arrival of these monstrous new weapons caused consternation within the city. In addition, several small earthquakes, followed by torrential rain, did nothing to raise the spirits of the defenders, who numbered only about 4000 Greeks and 2000 foreigners. The sole encouraging event was the arrival of the famous Genoese soldier, Giovanni Giustiniani, an expert in the defence of walled cities.

On Easter Monday, 2 April 1453, the first Ottoman troops arrived outside the walls. In less than a week, much of the outer wall had been destroyed by cannon fire, although the damage done each day was partly patched up in a makeshift manner by Giustiniani and his helpers at night, using wooden planks, old barrels and sacks filled with earth. Mehmed II determined to find a way to gain control of the Golden Horn, the natural harbour, without having to storm the defensive boom which the Christians had constructed across its entrance before the siege began. He decided on a startling plan of campaign. Wooden cradles were built and lowered into the water before dawn. Half his ships were floated on to the cradles and tied into position. With the aid of pulleys the ships were brought ashore, secure in their cradles. Teams of oxen and men pushed and pulled some 70 ships up and over the steep ground towards the shore of the Golden Horn. With oars flailing the empty air, trumpets sounding and flags flying, the remarkable proces-

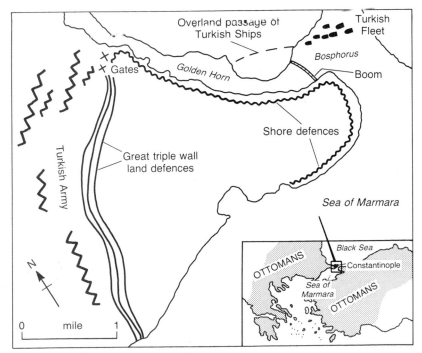

The siege of Constantinople, 1453

sion reached its destination. The defenders launched a night raid by fire-ships in an attempt to rid themselves of their unwelcome visitors, but the plan was betrayed and a number of Christian ships were sunk. Throughout early May the bombardment of the city continued, supplemented by Ottoman attempts to dig tunnels and undermine those walls which were still standing. The Ottomans also brought into use wooden towers on wheels, protected on the outside by bullock hides and camel skins. Inside each tower was a ladder leading to a platform the height of the outer wall. The towers were intended to give shelter and protection to the soldiers filling in the fosse to make a pathway across to the outer wall, but after the defenders had set fire to one under cover of darkness, causing considerable loss of life, the towers were withdrawn from use.

The plight of the defenders became serious. Few had been killed, but many had been wounded and all were suffering from hunger, as provisions were running low. Morale was seriously affected by a series of events: unseasonable thunderstorms, torrential rain, an eclipse of the moon, and an accident to the city's most venerated icon while it was being carried in procession. The Ottomans too became pessimistic about the outcome of the siege, and the Sultan even opened negotiations with the Emperor. But these came to nothing. The Emperor refused to surrender on terms. In consequence, Mehmed ordered an all out attack on the city. When everything was ready, he summoned his commanders and spoke to them of their sacred duty as followers of Islam to take the city from the Christian infidels. The city was, he said, not impregnable, and, despite the hard times on which it had fallen, held many opportunities for plunder. At the same time, inside the city, the Emperor was speaking to the assembled citizens about the expected assault and urging them to fight for the True Faith against the Moslem infidels.

The final attack began suddenly in the early hours of 29 May. At first, wave after wave of attackers were repulsed, but at sunrise the end came suddenly and unexpectedly. Giustiniani, the Christian commander, was badly wounded. He lost his nerve and begged his companions to remove him from the battlefield. His bodyguard carried him through a small gate in the walls down to a Genoese ship. The Genoese soldiers he had brought with him saw him go and, before the gate could be shut again, they streamed through it after him. At about the same time a party of some 50 Janissaries found a small gate, which had been left unbarred. They pushed their way into the courtyard beyond and up the steps to the top of the wall where they hoisted their flag. Panic broke out among the defenders all along the wall. The Emperor was cut down and killed in the ensuing confusion inside the city. Later stories say that his head was cut off, as was the Ottoman custom with prisoners, and taken to the Sultan who had it embalmed and sent on exhibition round the Islamic world. A headless body, found later, was identified as that of the Emperor by the Byzantine imperial eagle embroidered on its socks. Mehmed II was not only the conqueror of Constantinople, but had become the successor to the last Greek Emperor. He is said to have walked in melancholy mood through the ruins of the imperial palace and to have quoted the words of a Persian poet: 'The spider is the curtain holder in the palace of the Caesars and the owl hoots its night call on the towers . . .' Some of the defeated Christians managed to reach their remaining ships, which were still anchored near the boom, and made good their escape.

Within the city there followed the customary three days of unrestricted plunder, pillage, rape and murder allowed to the soldiers (and sailors) by Islamic law in any city which had refused the chance to surrender and had had to be taken by force. For that time the streets literally ran with blood. Later, prisoners were taken to become slaves. The imperial palace was sacked, books and icons were burnt, jewels were seized, and marbles and mosaics were smashed. Churches were stripped of their treasures, warehouses and storerooms along the Golden Horn were emptied of their goods and the shops in the bazaar were ransacked. The civilians who had sought sanctuary in the great cathedral of Hagia Sophia (Holy Wisdom) were rounded up and killed. Private houses were plundered and their contents were carried off as legitimate spoil, together with their owners.

At the end of the three days, Mehmed restored order and set about the task of rebuilding the city, which he now renamed Istanbul, the Ottoman version of the Greek words 'stin poli' meaning '(in) the city'. Hagia Sophia was transformed into a mosque, Aya Sofia. A new palace was constructed and houses and shops were rebuilt. The city prospered and within a century its population had risen to 750000, making it one of the largest cities in Europe.

a) Sources of Information

How do we know so much about the fall of Constantinople? We are fortunate in having first-hand accounts of what happened from a number of contemporary sources. The most detailed, and probably the most reliable, was written by a Greek, George Phrazantes, who was actually present in the city during the siege, and who wrote his account fairly soon after the events which he described. He had married into the Byzantine Imperial family and had become a confidante of the Emperor. He was well placed to know what was going on, and wrote it down in a vigorous and apparently unbiased narrative.

Most other European chroniclers only wrote about the siege years later, and most of them had not been present at the events they described. An exception was Nicolo Barbaro, a Venetian ship's doctor, who kept a diary which gives us a good chronological framework of events, while another man, a Genoese priest, who was also in the city, wrote his story down only six weeks after the city was captured and while it was still fresh in his mind. All these sources, of course, give an account of events from a European point of view, and their sympathies are naturally with the embattled Christian defenders. Unfortunately, Ottoman sources are sparse and disappointing. Even the best of them was not written down until more than a century after the event.

b) Effects on Europe

A fortnight after the fall of Constantinople the news reached Crete. It was brought by three of the ships which had escaped from the Golden Horn. It was received with horror, 'there never had, and never will be a more dreadful happening'. By the end of June refugees were arriving in Venice. In mid-July the news arrived in Naples and Rome, and from there spread to the rest of Europe.

The unthinkable had happened; Constantinople, the great Christian city, the eastern equivalent of Rome, was in Moslem hands. A Crusade seemed the answer. The Pope and the Holy Roman Emperor began to plan accordingly. Most of the European nobility were lukewarm about another crusade against the Ottomans, remembering the crushing defeat at Nicopolis in 1396. The thunderings of the Bishop of Siena brought no response either: 'Already Mehmed rules among us, already the sword of the Turks hovers over our heads, already the Black Sea is closed to us. Meanwhile we live in discord and enmity . . . How much better if we were to turn our swords against the enemies of our faith'. The Christian powers of Europe failed to act effectively to rescue Constantinople, because they simply were not willing to join together and fight in defence of their faith. Profitable trading opportunities with the Ottoman Empire enjoyed by many Christian rulers led them to draw back from military confrontation with the Sultan. As a result of his capture of Constantinople, Mehmed was able to forge ahead with further conquests. One after another of the former territories of the Byzantine Empire fell victim to his armies, and by the end of 1461 the Byzantine Empire was no more (see Map, p. 14 and also Chapter 2 for details of Mehmed's conquests).

How had the Ottomans reached the point that they could so threaten Europe? Who were they and where had they come from?

2 Beginnings of the Ottoman State

On the highest hill in Istanbul stands the Suleimaniye, the great mosque built by Suleiman the Magnificent to the design of his famous architect, Sinan, and completed in 1557. The mosque has ten galleries and four minarets from which the faithful are called to prayer. Sinan did not choose these numbers at random. They are an allusion to the fact that Suleiman was the tenth Sultan of the Ottoman dynasty and the fourth to rule over the city since its conquest in 1453.

Suleiman traced his descent from Osman (or Othman), the founder of the Osmanli or Ottomans, who ruled, in the first quarter of the fourteenth century, over one of the small frontier states in western Anatolia (modern Turkey). The origin of these states is to be found in the steppe lands of Central Asia, where lived a number of nomadic tribes (Turcomans). These people were gradually pushed further and further westwards by successive Mongol migrations. They were warrior societies, ruled over by hereditary chiefs, to whom all members owed personal loyalty. Some of them settled in oases near the Caspian Sea and began to trade animals, furs and captives with the Moslems to the south and west. The Turks had earlier come into contact with Moslems in the course of border raids and in chance encounters with wandering Moslem holy men, but it was the commercial contacts with Moslem traders which seems to have been the most influential in converting them to Islam. By the end of the tenth century Islam was firmly established among them.

Soon after this they began, in the service of the Seljuk war lords, to move into Moslem territory to the south. The Seljuks, with the Turks in their wake, overran Persia and then moved west into the Islamic heartland, taking over the important religious centre of Baghdad in 1055, and setting up their own Islamic empire. The Turks enjoyed a life of fighting, and were unwilling to settle down for long. In the course of the twelfth century they began to advance into western Anatolia, raiding and plundering land which still belonged to the Byzantine empire. It was an added bonus for the Moslem Turks that this warfare against non-Moslem neighbours could be given a cloak of respectability, for it was their sacred duty, laid down in the Koran, to extend Moslem territory (*Darulislam*, 'Abode of Islam') into the land of non-Moslems (*Darulharb*, 'Abode of War'). The goods captured in a raid (*ghaza*) against Christians were, according to the religious laws of Islam (*sheriat*), lawful booty and any prisoners taken could be killed or made into slaves. Their raids became more frequent and adventurous as time went by, and by the middle of the thirteenth century western Anatolia was almost entirely in the hands of Turkish *ghazi emirs* (princely warrior chiefs), like Osman. His emirate was small and insignificant, but it was the one which survived and absorbed all the others to become the Ottoman Empire (see page 11).

3 Ottomans and Turks

In most western historical writings 'Turkish' and 'Ottoman' are used interchangeably, as if they had the same meaning. But there is an important difference, since most Turks were not Ottomans (and most Ottomans were not Turks).

'Ottoman' originally had a purely dynastic meaning – the family and descendants of Osman – but it quickly came to include his followers and supporters whether or not they were related to him by blood (rather as members of a Scottish clan took the surname of their chief although they were not his blood relations). Later the name came to have an additional social and cultural meaning. To be an Ottoman was to be a member of a privileged élite within the *askeri* (military/ruling) class, whose advanced education and lengthy training set them apart from other members of the *askeri* class.

In order to 'be an Ottoman' one had to satisfy three conditions: to serve the state, to serve the faith and to 'know the Ottoman Way'. To serve the state meant working for the government in a position of civil or military responsibility and prestige; serving the faith meant simply being a Moslem, and observing the teachings of Islam, while 'knowing the Ottoman Way' meant having a full understanding and knowledge of the High Islamic tradition. This involved a lengthy education in all the political, administrative, legal, financial and educational aspects of Moslem civilisation and culture as it had developed over the centuries. It necessitated absolute religious orthodoxy, acceptance of a rigid class structure, and behaving at all times in strict accordance with traditional Moslem manners and customs. In addition, it required a fluent knowledge of Osmanli, the Ottoman language, which was based on Turkish but with a large admixture of Arabic and Persian. It was used as the language of government and was totally incomprehensible to ordinary Turks. An Ottoman would also be able to speak, read and write in Persian (for poetry) and Arabic (for religion).

How did one become an Ottoman? The easiest route for a boy born a non-Moslem was via the *devshirme* (the tribute of Christian boys paid by Ottoman territories in the Balkans – see page 66). He would become a Moslem and receive suitable education through the palace system, enabling him to become either a Janissary (which would at least ensure him a place in the *askeri* class) or a bureaucrat in central or provincial government (which would ensure him a position within the Ottoman élite). The same procedure would be followed by non-Moslems who entered the system as prisoners of war or through the slave markets.

For a boy born a Moslem (but not into the *askeri* class) it was much more difficult. It is true that he was already of the right religion, but rising from the *reaya* (the subject class) presented problems, which could only be solved by finding an Ottoman sponsor early enough to make the proper education possible. This was extremely difficult to do. In the early days of the empire, a young Moslem volunteer might be able to distinguish himself by fighting with the sultan's army, being awarded a *timar* and thus becoming a feudal *sipahi* and a member of the *askeri* class. But this did not happen often, and, after the early sixteenth century, almost never. There was a further problem for a boy born a Moslem, even for a boy born into the *askeri* class. Most Ottomans who were members of the Sultan's household in the broadest sense, were slaves (at least from the early fifteenth to the late sixteenth century). Anyone born a Moslem could not be a slave. The path of promotion for a Moslem-born boy, therefore, was normally via the *ulema* (the religious establishment) through which he could become a teacher, judge or scribe. Membership of the *ulema* did not, however, carry the same authority or prestige as government service, and was regarded as second best. It used to be thought that *no* free born-Moslem could be employed in direct government service in the sixteenth century. Recent research has shown that this was not so. It was often the case that, after the right education, boys born into the *askeri* class were helped by their fathers' influence to find good careers in central or provincial government, thus short-circuiting the slave system. By the mid-seventeenth century the end of the *devshirme* (slave) system meant that the admission of Moslem boys into direct government service became usual.

To summarise the Ottoman–Turk relationship:

1. The Ottomans were the ruling élite, part of the *askeri* (military) class, usually European by race, Christian-born and converted to Islam, educated, small in number, slaves, but great in power and exempt from taxation. They spoke Osmanli.

2. Moslem-born members of the *askeri* class were, until the mid-seventeenth century, either members of the *ulema* (the religious hierarchy) or were feudal *sipahis*. They were free.

3. The Turks were Turcomans, Moslem-born Anatolian peasants by race, illiterate, poor, numerous, freeborn but without power, part of the tax-paying *reaya*. Largely tied to the land. They spoke Turkish, and were looked down upon by the Ottomans.

4 The tax-paying peasants of the Balkans, made up of the *reaya*, Moslem-born Turks forcibly resettled there, and the *zimmis*, non-Moslem Slavs, Greeks and others. Free but largely tied to the land.

4 The Empire Develops

The emirate of Osman, in north-west Anatolia, and bordering on the Byzantine defences of Constantinople, faced greater dangers than the other emirates in the region. That it maintained and extended its frontiers was due to the leadership of Osman. His name spread after he and his *ghazis* defeated a large Byzantine army in 1301. *Ghazis* from other areas, with their leaders (*beys*) came to join Osman in large numbers. They accepted his leadership and gave him their absolute loyalty, in return for which he led them on raids which provided them with plunder.

a) First Steps in Europe

Osman and his son Orhan captured city after city in northwest Anatolia. One of them, Bursa, became their capital, and today is still noted for the mosques which they built. In 1336 they gained possession of a neighbouring emirate, which gave them lands on the Marmara and Aegean coasts. Now the way to Europe lay open – only a few miles away, across the Dardanelles.

Within a few years the Byzantine Emperor, in the throes of a civil war, was asking the Ottomans for military aid. The first Ottoman adventure in Rumelia ('land of the Romans' as they called it) had begun. All was well until, when the campaign ended, the Ottomans refused to leave the bridgehead they had established near Gallipoli. In 1354 a series of earthquakes destroyed most of Gallipoli and several nearby towns. As the inhabitants fled from the devastation, the Ottomans, who were still camped in the neighbourhood, moved into the wrecked cities, which they fortified and garrisoned with reinforcements from Anatolia. The Ottoman frontier had been shifted permanently into Europe. But it did not remain static for long. As the Ottomans advanced into the Balkans during the next thirty years, the newly conquered lands were quickly colonised by Turks brought over from Anatolia. The capital was moved from Bursa to Edirne (Adrianople) that is, from Anatolia to Europe. Ottoman intentions were clear. They were in Europe to stay.

b) Patterns of Conquest

Geographical conditions helped the early Ottoman conquests in Europe. Despite the mountains, routes for the passage of armies were not hard to find. All important was the valley of the River Danube. Once the Danube had been reached anywhere above the Iron Gate (see Map, page 14) the way west to Hungary and Central Europe lay open. Invaders could easily turn east, enter Moldavia and Wallachia, and then move on towards the Black Sea coast.

The Ottomans' three-pronged attack had led them west, by an old routeway towards Albania and the Adriatic coast, south, into Greece to the port and city of Salonika, and, north along the road to Belgrade, over the mountain passes to Serbia, and into Bulgaria. By the end of the fourteenth century they controlled all the main routes into the Balkans. As they had done at Gallipoli, they brought peasants from Anatolia to settle along these highways, and to work the land. The frontier areas were particularly densely populated by these Turkish immigrants and provided a firm base for Ottoman rule.

The Ottomans had the advantage during this period of conquest, not only of favourable geographical conditions, but of political instability in the Balkans. The Byzantine empire had been in decline there since a policy of devolution, the handing over of power to local rulers, had begun in the early fourteenth century. These near-independent rulers, the Despots, controlled most of Greece. The authority of the emperor was further reduced by a series of dynastic struggles – at one time there were four different 'emperors' in Constantinople struggling for power.

By 1400, as a result of Ottoman conquests, only Macedonia and Thrace remained under direct Byzantine rule, and the emperor had become an Ottoman vassal.

The Ottomans were not alone in taking advantage of Byzantine fourteenth-century weakness. The Serbs at first also benefited. Their empire was founded in the 1350s by Serbian conquests of Macedonia, Albania and Epirus, while royal family connections gave them control over Bulgaria. The king of Serbia proclaimed himself Emperor of the Serbs and Greeks. But his empire did not long outlive him. Under his weak successors, it disintegrated and fell as easy prey to the other major political force in the Balkans, Hungary. Louis the Great, who was also king of Poland, took full advantage of the chaotic conditions in Serbia and by 1380 had seized Dalmatia, Bosnia, northern Serbia and north-eastern Bulgaria, and forced Moldavia and Wallachia to recognise him as overlord. These conquests provided Hungary with a buffer-zone against the Ottoman advance, at least for a time.

A further complication in the Balkans was the presence of a number of firmly established, but rival, Genoese and Venetian trading posts in Greece and on the islands of the Aegean (see map, page 14).

As well as geographical and political advantages, the Ottomans had the determination and drive, backed by the military strength of the Janissaries (see page 69) to achieve order out of chaos, and to become the overall victors in the Balkans by the middle of the fifteenth century.

There were two stages in the Ottoman conquest of new lands. Firstly, they established some degree of political control, usually in the form of overlordship. Having subdued the territory, the Ottomans would set up a new ruling family, usually chosen from among the compliant local nobility, with the status of tribute-paying vassal. The tribute usually took the form of providing troops for Ottoman campaigns whenever required, in return for which the vassal retained independence and a political identity for his lands. Some Balkan lands, Wallachia, Moldavia and Transylvania, remained as vassal states and were not directly incorporated into the Ottoman empire, but usually the second step was to remove the vassal ruler, annex the territory to the Ottoman Empire and establish direct political control. This included introducing the *timar* system (see page 73) which provided a supply of well-equipped cavalry troops, who were also responsible for provincial administration and tax collecting.

It was fortunate for the Ottomans that they faced no major opposition in the Balkans during the early period of conquest. If they had, the situation would have been very different, for the Ottomans were often very vulnerable, with long supply and communication lines which could easily be cut or disrupted. Why was there so little opposition? The peasantry throughout the Balkans had been severely oppressed by their feudal overlords. Where direct Ottoman rule was introduced, they benefited from what in most cases was a much more tolerant régime.

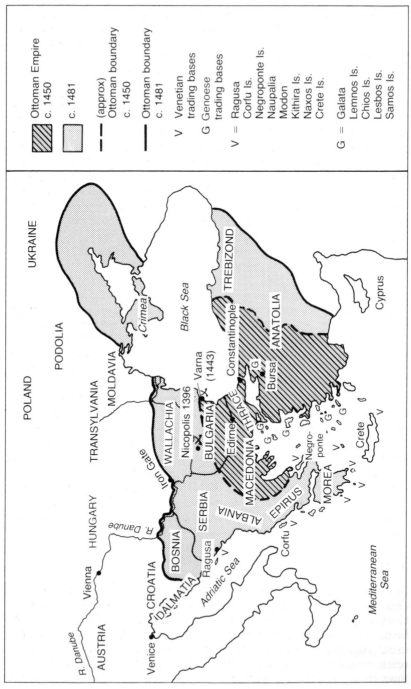

Political Geography of the Balkans, 1450–81

Taxation was fairer and less severe. Labour services were reduced and no longer dependent on the whim of the landowner. By the later fourteenth century, the Ottomans had imposed a strongly centralised and well organised government which operated to the advantage of the peasants. The government attitude to non-Moslems was tolerant. The Orthodox Church, to which most of the peasants were devoted, was officially recognised, and although the Catholic Church, to which most of the nobility adhered, was suppressed, there was little religious persecution, and no pressure (other than some tax advantages) to convert to Islam. Those nobles who openly opposed them were liquidated by the Ottomans, but others (a minority) who did not, were granted *timars* (see page 73). The peace and stability which Ottoman rule brought to the Balkans (Pax Ottomanica) was welcome after the weak rule and political chaos of the preceding century or more. Although it also brought with it certain disadvantages, these, despite the horrors depicted by contemporary western propaganda, were, on balance, outweighed by the advantages (see page 153).

c) Anatolia

In Anatolia the Ottomans used similar methods of conquest, although the situation there was complicated by religious considerations. Islamic law forbids waging war on fellow-Moslems, and the Sultan's military advance into eastern Anatolia was strongly objected to by the Karamanids. They were Turcoman tribesmen who had settled in the old Seljuk capital of Iconium.

Difficulties with the Karamanids, at the same time as a Balkan revolt erupted in 1388, highlighted a serious problem which was to beset the Ottomans and which they never satisfactorily solved: the Ottoman Empire was a two-front state with a one-front army. Unrest in either the Balkans or in Anatolia while a campaign was being waged in the other, meant a hasty end to the current conflict in order to transport troops, equipment and, most important, the Sultan to the other front. The Sultan had to lead his army in person to maintain the image of the great *ghazi* leader, continually extending the Abode of Islam into the Abode of War.

d) Disaster at Ankara

In the late fourteenth century, Bayezid I, having successfully extended Ottoman power in both Anatolia and the Balkans, planned to capture Constantinople, in order to unite the two halves of his Empire. In 1394 he began the siege. A crusade to save the city was launched, amidst the usual bickerings, by western Europe. The crusading army finally reached Buda and set sail down the Danube. Bayezid moved swiftly towards Constantinople and cut off the crusaders at Nicopolis. There the Christians were totally destroyed in three hours in September, 1396, and there, with them, died the last real crusade.

Bayezid's reputation as 'The Thunderbolt' was enhanced by this victory and he followed it up by annexing the Karamanid lands in Anatolia. By 1398 he controlled almost all of the Byzantine Empire, apart from Constantinople, the siege of which was still going on. He might well have succeeded in its capture eventually, if he had not been distracted from the task by the arrival on the scene not of an army from the west, but an outstanding warrior and adventurer from the east. Timur Lenk (Timur the Lame), known to the west as Tamburlaine, had built up an empire for himself by subjugating most of Persia and then invading Anatolia. A clash with Bayezid was inevitable. In June 1402 it took place near Ankara. The Ottomans were defeated and Bayezid was taken prisoner. He died a year later, leaving the Ottoman Empire a part of Timur's domains.

However, he left behind him an important legacy, in the centralised government he had developed, and in his transformation of the Ottoman state into a traditional Islamic monarchy. On these foundations Mehmed the Conqueror and Suleiman the Magnificent would build.

e) Interregnum and Recovery

The decade from 1403 to 1413 is referred to by Turkish historians as the Interregnum. It was a time of troubles. When Timur died, Bayezid's sons began a struggle for power. It was finally won by the youngest son, Mehmed, who reunified the country and restored centralised government. The process was continued by his son, Murad II, under whose leadership further territorial gains were made in the Balkans, although an attempt to capture Belgrade failed, and efforts to bring Transylvania under direct Ottoman control were thwarted by the governor (the *voivode*).

Murad was a quiet man who became tired of war. He made peace in the Balkans and with the Ottomans' old enemies, the Karamanids in Anatolia, before abdicating in favour of his young son Mehmed, later known as Mehmed the Conqueror.

Making notes on 'The Ottoman Empire in the Mid-fifteenth Century;

This chapter is concerned with three main areas: the early history of the Ottoman empire (before 1450), the difference between Ottomans and Turks, and the fall of Constantinople. Start making a list of reasons why the conquest of Constantinople was important to the Ottomans.

You will find further information to add to your list as you read the next two chapters and Chapter 5. The following headings and sub-headings should help you make your notes on this chapter effectively:

1.   Fall of Constantinople
1.1. Sources of information
1.2. Effects on Europe
2.   Beginnings of the Ottoman state
3   Ottomans and Turks
3.1. How to become an Ottoman
4.   The empire develops
4.1. First steps in Europe
4.2. Patterns of conquest
5.   Anatolia
5.1. Disaster at Ankara
5.2. Interregnum and recovery

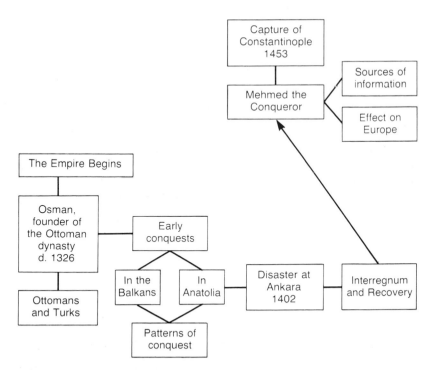

Summary – The Ottoman Empire in the mid-fifteenth century

Answering essay questions on The Ottoman Empire 1450–1700

The chapter which you have just read provides an introduction to the 'Ottoman Empire 1450–1700'. It contains useful background material that you need to understand, but it is very unlikely that you will have an opportunity to include detailed information on the early Ottoman conquests or on the capture of Constantinople in 1453 in an answer to an A-level essay question.

The difference between Ottomans and Turks is something that you will need to keep in mind throughout your work on the Ottoman empire. As you read through the rest of this book you will notice that the words 'Turk' or 'Turkish' are rarely used, and then only with reference to modern Turkey. Unfortunately, A-level examiners do not always make the distinction between Ottoman and Turk, and they continue to ask questions about the 'Turkish empire' and about the reasons why the 'Turks' were so successful. This western European practice dates back to at least the sixteenth century, when 'Turk' became an all embracing pejorative term covering Ottomans, North Africans, and Moors as well as the Turcomans of Anatolia, and when the Ottoman sultan was referred to as the 'Grand Turk'.

Individual A-level questions on the Ottoman empire are unlikely to cover the whole of the period 1450–1700. They almost invariably fall into one of three categories: the rise (or expansion) of the empire, the decline of the empire, and the achievements of the best known of the sultans, Suleiman the Magnificent. You will find 'Answering essay questions' sections on these three main topics at the end of the relevant chapters.

CHAPTER 2

The Empire Expands 1450–1566

1 Mehmed the Conqueror (Fatih) (1451–1481)

The reign of Mehmed II (the Conqueror) begins a century of Ottoman expansion into Europe, Asia and North Africa, and a series of victories on land and sea. From the moment of his second accession to the throne in 1451 Mehmed embarked on a policy of aggression.

a) Europe

The conquest of Constantinople turned Mehmed into the most celebrated ruler in the Moslem world – and his new capital was the centre of that world. For the next 30 years he worked not only to make it into the most important and beautiful city in the whole world, but to make himself, as heir to the Byzantine Emperor, into the absolute ruler of an expanding empire.

In order to do this, he began to destroy everything that remained of Byzantine power. As a first step he ordered the murder of 'any among the Byzantine Greeks who could be named Emperor'. He followed this with campaigns directed against the surviving outposts of the Byzantine Empire. His fleet sailed into the Black Sea and compelled all the governments along its shores, including Trebizond, the Genoese trading bases in the Crimea and the Khan of the Golden Horde, to pay tribute in recognition of the Ottoman overlordship. This marked the transformation of the Black Sea into an 'Ottoman Lake', secured at its entrance by new fortifications on the Dardanelles.

*Between 1454 and 1464, Mehmed's armies drove deep into the Balkans south of the Danube, which he established as the Ottomans' northern frontier in south eastern Europe. In 1455 Mehmed overran Serbia and seized its valuable silver mines. The following year he attacked Belgrade, the obstacle barring his way to Hungary. He brought ships to blockade the city from the river and heavy guns to bombard it from the land, but before he was ready to storm it, relief forces arrived unexpectedly by night. Mehmed himself was wounded in the fighting which followed, and was forced to order a withdrawal.

Shortly afterwards a disputed succession to the Serbian crown gave Mehmed a chance to put forward his own claim to the throne. It was not a very strong claim, being based on his father's marriage to a daughter of the Serbian ruling house. The Serbians countered by putting forward plans for the marriage of a Serbian princess to a Bosnian prince. Such a marriage would unite and strengthen both countries, and make them a more formidable obstacle to Ottoman advance. Mehmed acted quickly to prevent the marriage, and settled the matter by force. Serbia was overrun in 1459.

* A drive by the Ottoman army into Greece gave them Athens in 1458 and the Morea in 1460. The conquest of the Morea brought the Ottomans into direct conflict with Venice, for the Venetians had important trading bases there. Hostilities began in 1463 on a trumped-up charge. The war dragged on for 16 years. For the first time, the Venetians found themselves at a disadvantage at sea. Until then Venice had been the undisputed naval power in the Mediterranean, but in the 1460s the Ottoman fleet proved itself to have not only numerical but technical superiority. The Ottomans' capture in 1470 of the island of Negroponte, the important Venetian trading base off the Greek mainland, was a crushing blow to Venice; the loss of this 'great island' threw the whole of Italy into a panic. Where would the Ottomans strike next? The answer was on the Adriatic coast where raids continued intermittently until, in 1478, Mehmed seized the great naval base of Scutari in Albania and in the following year reached the outskirts of Venice itself. The Venetians had no choice but to negotiate. They agreed to surrender their claims to a number of islands, including Negroponte, and to pay a substantial annual tribute to the Sultan. In return their right to trade with the Empire, which previous to the war they had enjoyed for many years, was restored, together with the right to keep a representative (*bailo*) in Istanbul again. A year later, in 1480, Mehmed's fleet sailed across the Adriatic and took the port of Otranto in southern Italy. From there he laid waste much of the surrounding area. The Italian states were to be left in no doubt who was the master of the eastern Mediterranean.

Bosnia was annexed in 1464. This completed the Ottoman domination of south eastern Europe, apart from the small Republic of Ragusa (Dubrovnik) which managed to retain its independence (see page 155). However, they still needed to establish full control over the Danube estuary in order to provide safe land communication with the Crimea, and in the northwest the Hungarians remained a threat. At the end of Mehmed's reign (1481) the Ottoman territories in the Balkans had been grouped together to form the second province (*beylerbik*) of the Empire. It was named Rumelia, the *Roman* lands. The first province was, of course, Anatolia.

b) Anatolia

In Anatolia (roughly the equivalent of modern Turkey, and sometimes called Asia Minor) Mehmed also established and extended his authority. In 1468 he annexed Karaman (the Karamanid capital). But this provoked stern resistance, with members of the Karamanid ruling dynasty carrying on guerilla warfare from the mountains with the help of local tribesmen. The Ak-Koyunlu ruler, Uzun Hasan took advantage of the situation to intervene in Anatolian affairs. He made a military alliance with Venice and launched a series of raids against Ottoman controlled areas in eastern Anatolia. The situation became so serious that Mehmed had to withdraw his forces temporarily from the Balkans. He mobilised his entire army of around 100000 men and defeated the forces of Uzun Hasan at Bashkent in 1472. The peace treaty which followed gave Mehmed control of the whole of Anatolia as far east as the River Euphrates.

*When he died in 1481 at the age of 49, Mehmed had achieved a great deal. But he left a number of ambitions unfulfilled. Among his current projects in the Mediterranean had been the conquest of the island of Rhodes, which he had attempted to take in 1480. In the same year he had made plans to follow up his success at Otranto in southern Italy, but he died before he could put his plans into effect. He had also begun, but had had to leave half-finished, a campaign against the Mamluk rulers of Egypt.

In the opinion of most modern Turkish historians, Mehmed was the true founder of the Ottoman Empire. He was the *ghazi* ruler who saw conquest as a way of life, and war as a necessity for effective government. Yet at the same time he was a tolerant and cultured man (see page 52).

2 Bayezid II (1481–1512)

a) The Jem Affair

Mehmed had made into law the old Ottoman custom that a Sultan should, on his accession to the throne, get rid of all possible rivals. The usual way of doing this was to order that all his brothers and their sons should be strangled with a silken bowstring. But when he died he left two sons, Bayezid and Jem. Each of them had been brought up in the tradition, as Mehmed himself had been, that princes should learn how to govern from an early age. Bayezid and Jem had both been put in charge of regions of Anatolia, and both were some distance from Istanbul. The sultanate would go to the son who could reach the capital first and could win the support of the Janissaries, the Ottoman standing army (see page 69) and the great officers of state. The Grand Vezir suppressed the news of Mehmed's death, and sent a secret message to Jem, whose succession he favoured. The secret became known and the Janissaries, who favoured Bayezid, 'kicked over the soup kettle', a signal for revolt, and murdered the Grand Vezir. At the same time, the messengers who had been sent to Jem were kidnapped before they could deliver their message. Bayezid arrived in Istanbul and was immediately proclaimed Sultan. When the news eventually reached him, Jem gathered an army to defy his brother, but was defeated by the Janissaries. He first fled to Egypt and afterwards to Rhodes. There the

Knights of St. John, who occupied the fortified city of Rhodes, saw him as a useful pawn against the Ottomans, with whom they were on bad terms. They sent him to safety in France while they negotiated for a substantial annual payment from the Sultan in return for making sure that Jem remained a prisoner.

Lengthy intrigues involving the Christian powers, the Pope and even the Moslem Mamluk rulers of Egypt led to the passing around of the luckless Jem from hand to hand. His involuntary travels only came to an end in 1495 with his death, which was a great relief to Bayezid as it removed the danger that a western coalition of Christian powers, using Jem as a figurehead, might invade the Ottoman Empire. No longer did he have to maintain strong defensive forces against such an invasion. He was now free to engage in a major offensive war.

b) Naval and Military Developments

In 1499 Bayezid declared war on Venice and, after several decisive Ottoman naval victories, captured the important Venetian trading posts of Modon, Coron and Lepanto in southern Greece. These battles took place in the open sea instead of close to the shore as had previously been the case, and marked an important development in the extension of Ottoman sea power. Bayezid was deeply interested in extending and modernising the Ottoman navy. The capture of Constantinople in 1453 had put into Mehmed's hands extensive dockyards, arsenals and naval supplies. But above all it had provided men who had the necessary expertise to turn the Ottomans from a people of the steppes into a people equally at home on the waters of the Mediterranean. Mehmed had begun to develop a fleet of galleys, and this was continued by Bayezid, who is credited by Turkish naval historians with designing a new type of fighting ship, which made provision on an upper deck to accommodate 40 soldiers. Certainly, Bayezid was the first Sultan to send a naval squadron into the western Mediterranean. He was responsible for the building of a new shipyard on the Golden Horn and for the rebuilding of the old one at Gallipoli. He brought in experienced foreign shipbuilders and seamen and used much of the one-fifth share of the booty from his campaigns, to which as Sultan he was entitled by Islamic law, to finance the work. By the end of his reign he had a large, modern and well equipped navy. The conquest of the three Venetian ports in southern Greece provided useful anchorages for the Ottoman fleet, and counterbalanced the recent acquisition by Venice of the strategically important island of Cyprus.

As well as improving the navy, Bayezid made changes in the army, reorganising it and introducing more firearms. He enlarged the Janissary corps, built a new training school and introduced a new system of selection. He decided on this course of action after a series of inconclusive campaigns against the Mamluks in the disputed border regions in the Tarsus Mountains of eastern Anatolia. In Europe, there was fierce sporadic guerilla fighting between Christian and Ottoman warlords all along the Danube, despite an eight-year truce.

c) European Politics

The Ottoman empire now began to play a part in the tangled web of European politics. Any state defeated in the Italian wars looked to the Sultan for help. Bayezid supported Naples and Milan against France and Venice and offered to send 25 000 soldiers if the port of Otranto, which had to be surrendered to Naples at the difficult time at the beginning of Bayezid's reign, was returned. The offer was not taken up. The Ottoman connection was to become increasingly important in the Franco-Habsburg struggle in the next century.

d) Anatolia

Bayezid's rule had been comparatively mild, initially because of the possibility that severity might lead to disaffection and to rebellion in support of Jem, but later because he seems by nature to have been a calm and contemplative man, who disliked violence. By 1511 it was clear that the ageing Sultan was losing his grasp on affairs of state. This encouraged rebellion among dissatisfied groups in Anatolia, particularly among heretical Moslem groups and among the Turkish nomads. These Turcoman tribes objected to the growing centralisation of Ottoman administration. Mehmed had tried to suppress them, but soon after 1500 the nomadic groups found a new political and religious leader, the charismatic Shah Ismail of Persia. Under him, they began to lay waste the Anatolian countryside as they marched towards the city of Bursa.

The situation was beyond the control of the Sultan, now old and ill. His son, Selim, with the support of the Janissaries, forced him to abdicate in April, 1512.

e) Assessment

Bayezid's reign is seen by Turkish historians as one of economic development in a period of comparative peace. The cities of Edirne and Bursa, two of the old Ottoman capitals, grew rapidly. Public buildings of all kinds were erected alongside the caravanserai, the inns providing free accommodation for the merchants and other travellers who used the trade routes on which the cities stood. As a contemporary of Bayezid commented, 'While he was not a great conqueror like his father, he consolidated the conquests of his father's reign.' By this period of tranquillity and by his modernisation of the army and navy, he created the conditions necessary for the fresh conquests of Selim I and Suleiman the Magnificent. Machiavelli was probably right when he wrote of Bayezid 'benefiting by the great achievements of Mehmed the Conqueror, and maintaining the Empire by the arts of peace rather than war; but if his successor, Selim, had been Sultan in the same mould, the Ottoman Empire would have been destroyed.'

3 Selim I (1512–1520)

Selim was the youngest of the three sons of Bayezid, but he had an important advantage over his brothers – because he was known to be strong and warlike in character, he was the favoured candidate of the Janissaries. During his father's lifetime he had been governor of the old Byzantine kingdom of Trebizond in Anatolia. There he had built up an army loyal to himself, well trained and experienced by being sent out to raid local supporters of Shah Ismail. Not content with this, Selim had asked for and eventually, by a display of force, had obtained from Bayezid a province in the central Balkans not far from Istanbul. This would give him an advantage when the struggle for the throne came. In an attempt to forestall what he believed to be a plan by one of his brothers to seize the throne in their father's lifetime, Selim marched on Istanbul with his army, but was defeated by Janissaries loyal to Bayezid. Plots and counter-plots followed in quick succession, before Bayezid was prevailed upon to abdicate in Selim's favour. Selim was proclaimed Sultan in April 1512. A month later Bayezid was dead. He was soon joined by Selim's elder brother and by five nephews. The remaining brother was taken prisoner in the course of a short civil war, and was subsequently killed on Selim's orders. Selim had taken Mehmed's law of fratricide to heart and was now undisputed ruler of the Ottoman Empire.

a) Anatolia

Selim began his reign by leading extensive raids against Shah Ismail's followers, 40000 of whom he had executed. He then denounced Ismail as a heretic, a *Shi'ite*. (The Ottomans were orthodox Moslems, *Sunnites*, and bitterly opposed to *Shi'ites*. This deep division among Moslems had originated in support of two different candidates to succeed the Prophet Mohammed.) Selim defeated Ismail in a decisive battle at Chaldiran near Lake Van in August 1514. This brought the frontier areas of Anatolia firmly under Ottoman control. As a result, not only was Anatolia now secure from attack, but the important routes to Azerbaijan, the Caucasus and Baghdad were open to the Ottomans. At the same time Selim extended his influence into Kurdistan. Most of the country was in his hands by 1516. Wisely he introduced a moderate policy of semi-autonomous government in the area, and so ensured loyalty from the local tribesmen.

b) The Mamluks

The extension of Ottoman power in eastern Anatolia, after Selim's defeat of Shah Ismail, led to an alteration of the balance of power between the Ottomans and the Mamluks. The Mamluks, who were a military ruling class descended from Turkish and Circassian slaves, had ruled Egypt and Syria for two and a half centuries. They, and the whole Arab world, were at this time alarmed by the arrival of Portuguese ships in the Red Sea and their attacks on shipping. In 1516 the Sherif of Mecca, the Islamic Holy City, proposed sending a deputation to Selim to ask for his help against the Portuguese, but the proposal was blocked by the Mamluk Sultan. When he heard what had happened, Selim marched against the Mamluks, announcing that he came both to save the Arab world from the oppressive yoke of the Mamluks and to defend it from the Portuguese infidel. He marched first against the city of Aleppo, where the governor and the people decided to surrender to him. In the battle which followed, the Mamluk Sultan and most of his army were killed. Afterwards, in the great mosque of Aleppo, Selim was proclaimed 'Servant of Mecca and Medina', one of the highest religious titles in the Islamic world. He then went on to take Damascus and Jerusalem, destroying the remaining Mamluk forces on the way.

Ottoman governors were appointed to each of the more important cities in Syria, and a strong garrison was stationed at Gaza to guard the route into Egypt across the Sinai desert. Selim was uncertain whether or not to continue the war. Egypt and Persia, were now separated by Ottoman-held Syria, and an anti-Ottoman alliance between them was unlikely. Persia had already been defeated; a campaign against Egypt was tempting. But an expedition across the Sinai desert would be dangerous. So he tried diplomacy, sending an ambassador to the newly proclaimed Mamluk ruler in Cairo to offer peace in return for Egypt agreeing to become an Ottoman vassal state. The Mamluk Sultan's reply was an unsuccessful attempt to recover Gaza, followed by the assassination of the Ottoman ambassador sent to Cairo. This affront determined Selim to attack Egypt. Early in January 1517, Selim set out and before the end of the month he had taken Cairo. The Mamluk Sultan was later captured and executed, and an Ottoman governor was appointed in his place. Any Mamluk resistance was at an end.

While Selim was still in Cairo, a large Portuguese fleet sailed into the Red Sea. It was driven back by an Ottoman naval force, much to the relief of the Sherif of Mecca who had been preparing to flee to the hills in the event of a Portuguese landing. In gratitude for his escape from danger, he sent Selim the keys of the Holy Cities of Mecca and Medina, in token that they had been put under the Sultan's protection. Syria, Egypt and the Hejaz (Arabia) had now all been added to the Ottoman Empire, and Selim was pressing a claim to part of the Yemen.

c) The Caliphate

Selim's reign marks a new development in Ottoman history. The addition of the Arab lands, particularly the Holy Cities of Mecca and Medina, transformed the Empire from a *ghazi* state into an Islamic Caliphate. It changed the status of the Sultan from a frontier ruler on the fringe of the Islamic world to the protector of Mecca and Medina, the guardian of the pilgrim routes to and from the Holy Cities, and the possessor of the holy relics of the Prophet Mohammed, the symbols of the caliphate. He bore the title of Caliph, although he was not, in the classical sense, the caliph of the whole Islamic world. This would have been impossible for, according to orthodox Sunni Moslem doctrine, *the* caliph, as successor to the Prophet, had to be from the Prophet's own tribe. Suleiman I later laid claim to the 'Supreme Caliphate', but he was only emphasising his pre-eminent position among Moslem rulers, and his role as protector of the whole Islamic world. He was not claiming descent from the Prophet Mohammed.

The Ottoman Sultans always remained *ghazi* sultans as well as caliphs, and viewed the caliphate in terms of *Jihad* (Holy War). They were the official 'Protectors of Islam', but for them that duty of protection was not defensive or passive; it was always aggressive. 'The world must be one, with one faith and one sovereignty'. One result of this change in the position of the Ottoman Sultans within the Islamic world was to raise the *sheriat* (religious law) to a position of supreme importance in the administration of the Ottoman state.

d) Europe

The Balkans remained quiet throughout Selim's reign, apart from the incessant and unofficial raids and counter-raids along the Danube frontier. Selim renewed the truce with Hungary, which had already been extended several times, and he also renewed the commercial privileges of Venice within the Empire. On payment of an annual tribute, Venice retained possession of Cyprus, which had previously been held from the Mamluk Sultan, as well as trading rights in Syria and Egypt which he had granted to them.

Although Selim made no aggressive moves against Europe, the Ottomans still remained a threat there. At the end of his reign it was confidently believed that he was planning to launch an attack on the island of Rhodes, but before he could carry out any such plan he died, in September 1520.

e) Assessment

Over the years Selim has been the subject of very different judgements. Turkish historians know him as Selim *Yavuz* (the Grim), because of his habitual severity of manner and his fierce outbursts of anger. He was the *ghazi* leader par excellence, full of warlike vigour, forever on campaign. Yet he was also a patron of learning, highly literate himself and a writer of poetry. He was keenly interested in both the world around him, and, unlike most Ottomans, in the world beyond the frontiers of his Empire. Presented with a *mappa mundi*, a map of the then known world, he considered the possibilities which it raised for further conquests. It is thought that he planned the conquest of India, where the Sunni Moghul empire was a tempting prize, but, if so, death intervened before he could proceed with it. He certainly sent observers as far as China to bring him reports of that country.

A fellow poet and contemporary Ottoman historian, who had accompanied him on his Egyptian campaign, wrote in a lament for Selim's death, that, in a brief space of time he had achieved much and like the setting sun, had cast a long shadow on the face of the earth. His son, Suleiman the Magnificent, was to reap the benefit of Selim's conquests in the east, which had opened up the trade routes and doubled the state's annual income, leaving at his death a full Treasury. The words of a contemporary are perhaps Selim's best epitaph – 'The Sultan that lifteth up the flags of Islam to the sky of glory'.

4 Suleiman I (the Magnificent, the Law Giver) 1520–1566

Suleiman, Selim's only surviving son, was one of the few Ottoman Sultans to succeed to the throne without the need to shed blood. Under him Ottoman ambitions were again focussed on the west, where the European political situation was dominated by the power struggle between the Habsburg Charles V, King of Spain and Holy Roman Emperor, and the Valois Francis I, King of France. Standing on the side lines was the Tudor Henry VIII, King of England.

From the Ottoman point of view, the Valois–Habsburg rivalry was greatly to the Empire's advantage. When Charles took Francis prisoner at Pavia in northern Italy in 1525, the French sought aid from the Ottomans. Both the French and the Ottomans saw an alliance as the best means of preventing the domination of Europe by a single power. The French ambassador told Suleiman in 1526 that if Francis were to accept Charles's conditions, Charles would become 'the ruler of the world'. The Franco-Ottoman alliance became an integral part of European power-politics, and the threat of Ottoman advances towards central Europe became an important factor in the spread of Protestantism in that region (see page 159). Ottoman policy was firmly based by Suleiman on support for anti-Habsburg elements. These included not only France and the German Protestants, but also the Moriscos of Spain. In North Africa too there were opportunities for anti-Habsburg activities through the Moorish corsairs of the Barbary coast (see page 32).

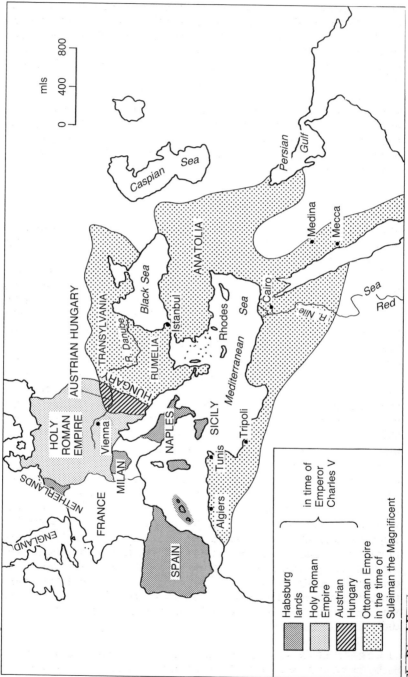

Map legend:

Habsburg lands	in time of Emperor Charles V
Holy Roman Empire	
Austrian Hungary	
Ottoman Empire in the time of Suleiman the Magnificent	

The Rival Empires

From the accession of Suleiman to the end of the century, there was no question of European international politics which did not somehow involve the Ottomans. However, towards the end of this period conditions changed. The Peace of Cateau–Cambresis had brought to an end, for the time being, the Valois–Habsburg rivalry and had tipped the balance of power in favour of the Habsburgs, where it remained until the Treaty of the Pyrenees a century later in 1659, while the second half of the sixteenth century saw France involved in a long religious civil war. As a result, she ceased to be the Ottoman ally in Europe. At the same time the death of Suleiman brought about the beginning of changes within the Ottoman Empire itself, and its relations with the west.

a) The Eastern Mediterranean

Suleiman began his reign with two objectives, both of which his predecessors had failed to achieve – the conquest of the city of Belgrade and of the island of Rhodes.

Rhodes was the necessary base for maintaining Ottoman naval supremacy in the eastern Mediterranean and protecting the trade routes with Egypt. The island had been in the hands of the Knights of St. John of Jerusalem for over 200 years. The Knights were members of a religious order set up after the first Crusade to look after the Christian pilgrims to the Holy Land. They provided care for the sick and accommodation for the able-bodied travellers in their Hospitals, and came to be known as the Knights Hospitallers. The order was headed by a Grand Master, elected by the members, all of whom took religious vows and were then trained as soldiers and, later, as sailors. Increasingly, their religious purpose was subordinated to their military one, although they themselves would have seen the two elements as inextricably united in a holy war against the infidel.

With the capture of Acre in 1291 by the Moslems, the Knights were forced to leave the Holy Land. After finding temporary refuge on Cyprus, they settled permanently on the island of Rhodes, about fifteen miles off the coast of Anatolia. The city of Rhodes, which they fortified very heavily, proved to be an ideal place from which to harass Moslem shipping, and they soon gained a reputation as successful pirates, preying particularly on ships carrying pilgrims to and from Mecca and Medina. The problem became worse for the Ottomans after Selim had conquered the Mamluks, for the increased trade between Istanbul and the new provinces of Egypt and Syria proved irresistible to the Knights, whose island fortress lay close to the trade route. One Ottoman writer did not mince his words:

1 One sect of the accursed Franks, worst of the sons of error, sent by Satan and well-known for their cunning and falsity, outcasts,

damnable workers of wickedness, owned a great fortress . . .
inflicting great loss and suffering on peaceful merchants, captur-
5 ing or destroying their ships and carrying their crews off into
slavery. Rhodes was a sanctuary for these execrable Franks, and
here these damned souls had a secure base from which to send out
their swift galleys to the loss and hurt of Islam . . . enslaving and
10 imprisoning innocent people . . . How many sons of the Prophet
have been captured by these children of lies? How many
thousands of the faithful have been forced to deny their faith?
Their wickedness knows no end.

In 1521 Suleiman decided that the Knights' 'wickedness' should be
ended without further delay. At the end of September, the newly
elected Grand Master, Philip Villiers de Lisle Adam received a letter
from Suleiman calling on the Knights to surrender or face being put to
the sword 'by my large and victorious army'. After a lengthy exchange
of correspondence along predictable lines, Suleiman sent an ultimatum,
which read:

1 Your monstrous piracies which you continue to exercise against
my faithful subjects, and the insults which you offer to my
imperial majesty, oblige me to command you to surrender your
island and fortress immediately into my hands. If you do this, I
5 swear . . . that you shall be free to leave the islands, while the
inhabitants who remain there shall not be harmed. But if you do
not obey my order at once, you shall all pass under the edge of my
invincible sword, and the walls and fortifications of Rhodes shall
10 be reduced to the level of the grass that grows at their feet.

The ultimatum having been rejected, both sides prepared for action.
Suleiman assembled a large fleet of about 200 vessels at Istanbul, and
collected an army of probably something over 100 000 men from all
parts of the Empire. The number of fighting men on Rhodes totalled
about 2 500 of whom only 600 were Knights. Turkish historians
continue to say that there were more than 60 000 defenders within the
fort itself, but this would have been an impossible number. There
would not have been room for as many as that.
    The Ottoman ships sailed into Kalitheas Bay and disembarked troops
and guns which took up positions round the city. Skirmishes and
artillery fire followed until Suleiman himself arrived at the end of July
1522. The Ottomans used their 60 or so large cannon to fire huge stone
balls and primitive incendiary devices into the city, but these did only
slight damage, until they built a high earthwork from which the guns
could be fired with much greater accuracy. More serious for the
defenders was the Ottoman mining, – digging tunnels and shafts, and
exploding gunpowder under the city walls to make breaches in the

defences. By September, four fifths of the walls had been undermined. The Janissaries succeeded in storming a section of the ruined wall on several occasions. But they were driven back, as an English Knight wrote, 'after that the wall of the towne was downe, they gave us battell . . . yet thanked be God and St. John that at every battell they returned without their purpose'. At the end of November Suleiman ordered an all out attack. It was unsuccessful. 'Upon St. Andrew's Day was the last battell that was between the Turks and us . . . The Turks purposed to give us no more battell, but to come into the towne by trenches'.

In the middle of December Suleiman initiated tentative peace moves, which after much thought the Knights agreed to accept. A three day preliminary truce was declared, during which time no work was to be carried out by the Knights on the repair of the defences.

What happened next is disputed. Some western historians believe that de Lisle Adam was genuinely worried about Suleiman's good faith, and therefore sent a deputation asking the Sultan for an extension of the truce and further guarantees that the islanders would not be harmed after a surrender. Turkish historians accuse de Lisle Adam of duplicity, saying that he was merely trying to gain extra time to strengthen the city's walls, and that he had no intention of surrendering at all. The truce broke down, and fighting started again. The deadlock was broken by the islanders themselves, who, tired of seeing the daily destruction of their city, made their own peace overtures to Suleiman.

The terms of surrender offered were generous. The Knights were allowed twelve days in which to depart freely, taking their belongings with them, and with their honour untarnished. Suleiman even offered to provide ships to transport them if required. The safety of the islanders and their property was guaranteed. If any of them wished to leave during the next three years they could do so, but incentives to stay were offered in the form of tax exemptions, and most did stay. Suleiman, after meeting de Lisle Adam, expressed regret at being 'compelled to drive this brave old man out of his home', but on 1 January 1523 the Knights sailed out of the harbour in ships provided by the Pope. Among those who left was a young knight, Jean Parisot de la Valette. Forty five years later, when Suleiman attacked the Knights Hospitallers on their new island home of Malta, de la Valette was their Grand Master.

b) The Western Mediterranean and North Africa

With Rhodes in Ottoman hands, the eastern Mediterranean was safely under Suleiman's control. It was time to turn to the western Mediterranean and to the affairs of North Africa.

In the last years of the fourteenth century, *ghazi* warriors had sailed into the western Mediterranean and had established states in Algeria and Tunisia in order to provide a base for naval operations against the

Spanish monarchy, which was attacking their co-religionists, the Moors, in Spain. In the 1520s Spain seemed poised to realise a cherished aspiration, the conquest of Moslem North Africa. This was made possible by an alliance with Genoa, the possessor of a large and efficient fleet, and by military support from the garrison of Knights Hospitallers at Tripoli. As the greatest of the Moslem rulers, and, as Caliph, the protector of Islam, as well as overlord of Algiers, Suleiman could not stand by.

Thanks to the work of his father, Selim, Suleiman already had a well organised navy, excellent shipyards and plenty of labour. But he lacked experienced sea-captains. In order to remedy this, he turned to the corsairs, the pirates of the North African Barbary coast. These men were veteran sailors, trained and hardened by continual forays out of the port of Algiers against the Christians. Suleiman summoned their leader, Khair ad-Din (or Khaireddin), known to the west as Barbarossa, to Istanbul and put him in charge of the Ottoman navy. Barbarossa brought with him 18 of his captains, and, exercising the shipbuilding skills they had learnt from Portuguese captives, they built new and more up-to-date ships. Eight months later, in August 1534, Barbarossa sailed at the head of the Ottoman fleet to capture Tunis and to evict the Spanish vassal ruler, who had been installed there by Charles V. It was only a temporary victory as the Spanish recovered Tunis the following year, but it did indicate to the West the potential capability of the Ottoman navy under its new commander. This was borne out by Barbarossa's victory off the Albanian coast in 1538, against a combined fleet of Venetian, Spanish and Papal ships.

The next few years saw increasing co-operation between Barbarossa and Francis I. With the renewal of war between Francis and Charles V, Barbarossa was encouraged by Francis to ravage the coastal lands of southern Italy and Sicily looking for gold and other treasure, for corn and especially for men for the galleys. In 1543, he was with great difficulty persuaded by the French representatives, who accompanied him on his expeditions, not to raid the Papal States. A joint French-Ottoman fleet attacked and took the town of Nice, belonging to the Duke of Savoy, an ally of Charles. Afterwards, Barbarossa was allowed to winter his ships in the French port of Toulon, where, according to western sources, he and his men became a great nuisance to their hosts, plundering the countryside and carrying off peasants to man the galleys, whose crews had been decimated by disease. Turkish sources say otherwise, and that Barbarossa's men behaved impeccably. The following year, the war being over, the French asked them to leave, but they could only be prevailed upon to do so on payment of substantial sums of money.

Soon afterwards, in 1546, Barbarossa died at a great age, well into his eighties, and his place as the corsair leader was taken by Dragut. Ambitious and ruthless, he was made a captain in the Ottoman navy in

1551 and captured Tripoli from the Knights Hospitallers in the same year. The French, however, began to find their Ottoman naval allies unsatisfactory, for the Ottoman fleet proved unwilling to stay long in the western Mediterranean after the summer campaign was over. The French found themselves in the undignified position of having to follow the Ottomans east into the Aegean in order to keep in touch, and having to winter there.

In 1553 the combined fleets made an unsuccessful attack on the island of Elba in the western Mediterranean, after which Dragut retired, disgruntled, to Tripoli and took up his old life as a corsair. He and his followers became ever more active and daring, passing through the Straits of Gibraltar in search of Spanish treasure fleets, and seem even to have reached the Canaries. He became such a nuisance that Philip II of Spain sent a powerful force against Dragut's stronghold of Tripoli, where he now ruled as an Ottoman vassal. The Christians were, however, surprised and totally routed at the island of Djerba in May, 1560. This brilliant naval victory encouraged Suleiman to attack Malta.

c) Malta 1565

The Ottoman navy had seen little official action for several years, being confined to manoeuvres in the eastern Mediterranean, but in the spring of 1565 a formidable fleet left Istanbul for Malta and was joined by a force of corsairs, including Dragut, who was killed early in the siege. With his death the great age of the corsairs came to an end, for no one of the stature of Barbarossa or Dragut emerged to lead them. Although they continued to torment the Christian shores of the Mediterranean, they were too disorganised to present any serious threat.

The Knights of St. John (the Hospitallers) had been given sanctuary on the island of Malta by Charles V, 'in order that they might follow peacefully the rule of their order for the good of the Christian community, and at the same time use their forces and arms against the infidel enemies of the True Faith.' Malta was a very suitable base for the Knights. It was 1000 miles from Istanbul and reasonably safe from attack, while being conveniently placed for raiding shipping passing through the narrow part of the Mediterranean Sea between Sicily and North Africa. The Grand Master, Jean Parisot de la Valette was one of the Knights who had fought at Rhodes, and was now in his seventies (as was Suleiman). De la Valette was 'a very handsome man, tall, calm and unemotional, speaking several languages fluently, Italian, Spanish, Greek, Arabic and Turkish'. The last two he had learnt during a year as a galley slave.

When it became clear to the Knights that they were Suleiman's intended target, they strengthened the defences and provisioned the island for a long siege. The 700 Knights and the 8000 or so islanders awaited the armada of Ottoman ships, carrying probably 40000 men, arms and provisions under the command of yet another seventy year old, Mustafa Pasha. De la Valette told his men, 'The battle which is about to be fought will be the great battle between the Cross and the Koran. A formidable army of infidels will soon invade our island. As for us we are the chosen soldiers of the Cross, and if heaven demands that we sacrifice our lives, there can be no better time to do so than now'.

On 18 May, the Ottoman fleet sailed magnificently round the island and anchored eventually in the Bay of Marsa Scirocco. Within a few days, the army had disembarked and had occupied the southern half of the island. No immediate Ottoman attack was launched against the defences because of a difference of opinion between Mustafa Pasha and the naval commander as to what should be the primary target. Eventually it was agreed to move the fleet to the more sheltered harbour of Marsamuscetto, and to attack Fort St. Elmo with artillery fire from Mount Sciberras. For over a month the fort held out, until the ruined walls were finally overrun by the Janissaries.

The Knights in the fortified peninsulas of Senglea and the Borgo had relied on the guns of Fort St. Angelo to prevent enemy ships from entering the Grand Harbour, and so had not fortified the shores of French Creek. When they saw the Ottoman ships being dragged over Mount Sciberras from Marsamuscetto to the Marsa they were dismayed. Hastily, they made what preparations they could to resist a combined land and sea attack. The siege continued throughout the summer, and by early September both sides, after months of fierce fighting and heavy casualties, were near exhaustion. The Turkish army in particular suffered severely from disease, and was running short of ammunition and food. Morale was low. The Christians were little better, and were reported to be at their last gasp, when a relief force of 28 Spanish galleys arrived quite unexpectedly, and anchored unopposed in a bay on the north of the island. As soon as the news reached Mustafa, he organised the evacuation of the island. When he learnt that the Spanish forces numbered only 8000, half what he had been told, he turned back and prepared to fight. He was heavily defeated. His men, tired and dispirited, for once broke and ran, making for the safety of the boats. Fewer than 10000 would reach Istanbul.

The battle for Malta was over. The news of failure was not well received by Suleiman. 'I cannot trust any of my officers. Only in my own hand is my sword invincible', he is reported to have said. He never spoke to Mustafa Pasha again.

d) The Balkans

Belgrade

In 1521, the year after his succession, Suleiman marched against Belgrade in a carefully organised campaign. His predecessors had failed to take the city, which was the gateway to Hungary and to further expansion in the Balkans, and its capture was of prime importance to Suleiman. A combination of Janissaries, *sipahis* of the Porte and lightly armed mercenary horsemen (*akinjis*) surrounded and cut off the great fortress. Guns set up on an island in the Danube kept up a fierce bombardment, and a flotilla of Ottoman ships sailing upstream prevented any relief of the city by water. Internal quarrels among the defenders led to the surrender of the city at the end of August.

Hungary and the Battle of Mohaçs 1526
The Janissaries had been given very little to do for over three years, since the capture of Belgrade, and in 1525 a mini-uprising among them showed Suleiman that a new campaign must be quickly prepared.

The Grand Vezir Ibrahim, Suleiman's close friend, was recalled from Egypt where he had been sent as governor, and the decision taken to launch a massive offensive across the Danube in the spring of 1526. Bad weather then, as in all Suleiman's Balkan campaigns, made the march into Hungary difficult, and it took nearly six months for Suleiman and his army to arrive on the plain of Mohaçs in late August.

The young king of Hungary, Louis, was inexperienced as a military leader; the nobility was divided by bitter rivalries and unwilling to unite against a common enemy, and the Hungarian army was under strength, for many of the expected troops had failed to arrive. Nevertheless the Hungarians decided to stand and fight against a superior force on an open plain. To the east flowed the Danube, while to the south and west low wooded hills hid the Ottoman reserve troops.

The Hungarians took the offensive, their cavalry broke the ranks of *sipahis* and rode on into the formations of Janissaries and artillery. They were quickly surrounded, cut down and destroyed. Most of the nobility died in the rout. The King drowned under the weight of his horse which fell back on him while climbing the bank of a stream. Few ordinary soldiers survived. As an Ottoman historian wrote afterwards, 'The Janissaries aiming their arrows at the cruel panthers who opposed us, caused hundreds, or rather thousands to descend into hell.' Even today in Hungary, when disaster strikes, it is said, 'More was lost at Mohaçs'.

Suleiman pressed on to Buda, and then crossed the Danube to the twin city of Pest at the end of September. The campaigning season was nearly over, and he and his men began the march back to Istanbul, while in Hungary a dispute broke out over who should be the next king. Louis had been not only King of Hungary, but also King of Bohemia. His wife was a sister of the Archduke Ferdinand of Austria, who had himself married Louis's sister, Anna. When Louis was killed at Mohaçs, childless, Ferdinand claimed the inheritance, arguing that if the kingdoms of Hungary and Bohemia could be united with Austria, they would together form a powerful barrier against Ottoman aggres-

The Battle of Mohaçs

sion. Ferdinand had no trouble in talking his way to the Bohemian
crown, but in Buda he ran into difficulties. There he found that a rival
candidate, John Zapolya, the *voivode* (governor) of Transylvania, had
already been proclaimed King of Hungary. Ferdinand defeated
Zapolya, who turned to the Ottomans for help.

Suleiman, although he now believed that Hungary was his by right of
conquest, also believed that indirect control of the kind which he
exercised over vassal rulers in Wallachia and Moldavia would be easier
to maintain in Hungary than direct rule. A vassal ruler in Buda would
complete the ring of dependent states which protected his northern
frontier from the Black Sea to the Adriatic. Zapolya seemed a suitable
candidate. Suleiman therefore marched to Buda and invested him with
the kingdom of Hungary in return for his allegiance and the payment of

an annual tribute. Suleiman expressed to the ambassador of the Archduke Ferdinand his satisfaction with the arrangement:

1 This realm (Hungary) belongs to me, and I have set therein my servant. I have given him the kingdom, I can take it back from him if I wish, for mine is the right to dispose of it, and of all its inhabitants, who are my subjects. Let Ferdinand therefore
5 attempt nothing against it. What Janos Kral (King John Zapolya) does, he does in my name.

Vienna
In 1529 the weather was again bad when Suleiman and his army, and 22 000 camels to carry the provisions, left Istanbul in May for another Balkan campaign. Progress was slow, and it was July before they reached Belgrade and September when they arrived in Buda. Although the campaigning season was almost over, Suleiman decided to press on towards Vienna, and by the end of September was outside the gates of the city. Time was short, winter was approaching, Vienna must be taken quickly or not at all. Ottoman artillery failed to breach the walls, mining proved ineffective and the defenders held out. Vienna could not be taken, and on 14 October Suleiman gave the order to withdraw. His diaries reflect the appalling conditions. 'Snow from evening to noon next day . . . much loss of horses and men'. Quickly the Ottoman army struck camp, killed their prisoners, set fire to whatever they could not carry and marched away, while the bells of Vienna rang for joy. The most serious threat to Christendom had been averted.

Hungary Again
In the spring of 1532, the Ottoman army again set out from Istanbul for Belgrade, where elaborate preparations to welcome Suleiman had been made, including the construction of 'a rainbow arch'. He did not get to see it, for delayed by the resistance of an insignificant minor fortress, the Ottoman army had time only to raid the Austrian frontiers before marching wearily back to Istanbul at the end of the summer.

The following year Suleiman, who was anxious to begin a campaign against the Shah of Persia, made peace with the Archduke Ferdinand, who was equally anxious to end the long war. For the first time, Ottoman envoys were formally received in Vienna.

By the terms of the peace treaty, Hungary was to be divided between Ferdinand and Zapolya, along a line to be drawn by a Venetian representative, who was murdered three years later, while on a frontier demarcation mission. Ferdinand and Zapolya blamed each other for his death. The quarrel was eventually patched up, and an agreement made that on Zapolya's death, as he had no heir, his part of Hungary should pass to Ferdinand. Almost immediately, Zapolya most unexpectedly married Isabella, the daughter of the King of Poland. The following

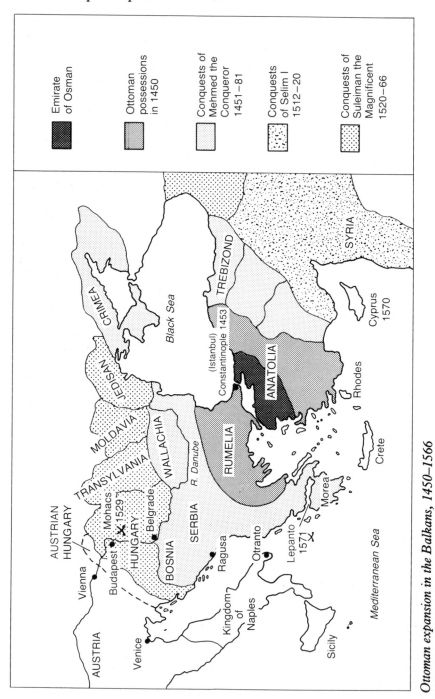

Ottoman expansion in the Balkans, 1450–1566

year, 1540, Zapolya died, shortly after the birth of a son (who was christened Stephen, but was later renamed John Sigismund). Despite this birth of an heir to Zapolya before his death, Ferdinand at once claimed the succession. Suleiman equally promptly marched into Hungary to settle the matter. He assured Isabella that her son should eventually rule Hungary, when he was old enough, but in the meantime she and the child were despatched to the Ottoman vassal state of Transylvania from which Zapolya had originally come. Despite his promise to Isabella, Suleiman briskly incorporated Zapolya's part of Hungary into the Ottoman Empire, putting it under direct rule. An Ottoman administration was set up, and churches were turned into mosques. After another Ottoman march (1543–4) into Hungary, Ferdinand was persuaded to pay an annual tribute of 30000 ducats, thus firmly establishing his status as an Ottoman vassal, for his share of Hungary.

In 1559 Isabella died, and her son John Sigismund began his rule as *voivode* of Transylvania at the age of 19. After the death of Ferdinand in 1564 his successor as Holy Roman Emperor, Maximilian II, not only delayed in paying the annual tribute for his share of Hungary, but became involved in a war with John Sigismund. When he heard the news, Suleiman set out for Hungary, on what was to be his last campaign, riding in a carriage instead of on horseback, old and ill. He received the homage of John Sigismud as his vassal, and assured him of full support against Maximilian, before going on to the siege of an unimportant town, Sziget. There the governor in an unexpected tribute to his enemy, had hung the walls with scarlet cloth and the tower with silvery material, before firing a salute to greet him. A month later the town fell, but Suleiman was already dead. The campaign ended abruptly, and the Ottoman army returned to Istanbul with the Sultan's body. The new Sultan had other interests than the Balkans. He renewed the earlier partition treaty with the Emperor, and peace of a sort came to Hungary for the next 30 years.

e) The East

The Mamluks
With the accession of a new, young and untried Sultan in 1520, the Mamluks, who had been incorporated into the Ottoman Empire by Selim I's conquest of Syria and Egypt, decided it was time to reassert their independence. Revolts broke out in both countries during the early 1520s. They were easily put down, but Suleiman decided that in Egypt there was need for a reorganisation of the administration. This task was entrusted to his Grand Vezir, Ibrahim, who successfully carried out a reform of justice, finance and administration along lines which gave Egypt firm and stable government for the next three centuries.

Persia

Suleiman had always recognised that his European enemies might seek to create a second front by uniting with the Persians in a simultaneous attack, and that in this lay his greatest danger. (In fact such a combined attack never took place, although it was several times proposed by both sides.) The Sultan was expected, indeed required, to lead his forces in person as the inheritor of the *ghazi* tradition, and the soldiers always fought better if he was present. If attacks came simultaneously from east and west he would not be able to do so. His armies could not easily be divided and it was difficult to find anyone to take the responsibility of acting as the Sultan's deputy to lead the second force, even if the sultan were prepared to diminish his authority by appointing a deputy. (During Suleiman's reign, however, there were occasions when Ibrahim was entrusted with command of part of the army, and in future reigns, as sultans ceased to lead their men personally into battle, it became common for the Grand Vezir to act as commander-in-chief.) As well as defending the Islamic world against its Christian enemies in the west, the Ottoman sultans had to deal with their fellow-Moslems, the Shi-ite Safavid rulers of Persia, who were always ready to attack the Ottoman Empire in the east.

The Ottoman frontier with Persia was ill defined. In the north of Anatolia, the tribesmen fluctuated in their allegiance between the Ottoman Sultan and the Persian Shah, depending on the situation at the time. Border warfare had been going on for years, made fiercer by the perpetual religious tensions betweeen the two countries.

Suleiman launched two full scale attacks, in 1533 and 1548, against the Persians. On each occasion he had to patch up some sort of peace in Europe before he could move his troops to the east. In 1533 the murder of the governor of Baghdad, who had offered his allegiance to Suleiman, gave the excuse needed. Ibrahim was sent on with an advance force to Kurdistan, where he took Tabriz without meeting any resistance. Suleiman joined him later, and after a long and difficult march over the mountains of western Persia, through deep snow and suffering from a shortage of food, they entered Baghdad on the last day of November, 1534, and there they spent the winter. (The Balkans were at an advantage compared with Persia in their contact with the Ottomans – it was too cold for the Ottoman army to winter in the Balkans, thus cutting short the campaigning season there; this, some historians would say, was the best defence which Vienna had.) The following summer was spent in fruitless pursuit of the Shah and his army, who steadfastly refused to stand and fight, being fully aware that in any set piece battle the Ottomans would be victorious. When Suleiman had unwillingly to return with his army to Istanbul, he was uncomfortably aware that he left the Shah's army intact.

As soon as Suleiman was safely back in his capital, the Shah recovered Tabriz and held it until 1548, the year of Suleiman's second campaign against Persia. It was brought about by the flight of one of the Shah's brothers to Istanbul. This suggested to Suleiman a possible weakening of the Shah's position which could be exploited. During this campaign, the Shah successfully employed the same military tactics as before, always keeping just out of reach of the Ottoman army and tempting them further and further away from their base. As Suleiman approached Tabriz, the Shah quietly abandoned it, rather than have to defend it in a decisive battle. Suleiman marched on towards the great fortress of Van, which quickly surrendered, and then moved to Aleppo, where he wintered his army. He spent the following summer in a series of raids, which brought much of the disputed border area under his control.

It was, however, extremely difficult for the Ottomans to keep direct control of such a remote and mountainous district from distant Istanbul. This meant that there was a practical limit to Ottoman expansion in the east. Realising this, Suleiman agreed to return Tabriz to the Shah in 1555 by the treaty of Amasya which set realistic limits for the eastern frontier, and which was destined to remain effective for the next 20 years or more. This left Suleiman free to turn his attention to more pressing European problems.

Russia

A new factor in middle eastern politics was the expansion of Russia, which began in the 1530s. Under Tsar Ivan IV, Russian armies advanced into the Moslem Khanates of the Volga basin, and reached Astrakhan by 1556. This threatened the Caucasus and the Black Sea, and created a situation which the Ottomans could not ignore. As he advanced south, laying the foundations of the Russian Empire, the Tsar collected allies among the Circassians. The *voivode* of Moldavia asked for his protection, and there was even an attempt to capture Azov, the northern outpost of the Ottoman Empire. Moslem pilgrims and merchants already found it difficult to travel through Persia on their way to Mecca and Medina from the north; now it looked as if routes along the Black Sea coast might become impassible as well.

The Ottomans had not previously thought the Russian expansion presented any danger, and had regarded the Russians as friendly neighbours, who as long ago as 1497 had been given permission to trade within the Ottoman Empire. Conditions were changing and Suleiman's successors would find that they had to take the Russian threat seriously.

*By the time of his death in 1566, Suleiman ruled all or part of modern Hungary, Yugoslavia, Albania, Greece, Bulgaria, Rumania, the Ukraine, the Crimea, Turkey, Iran, Iraq, Syria, Lebanon, Jordan, Egypt, Libya, Tunisia, and Algeria, with a total population of more than 20 million. He was the *Padishah* (Shah of Shahs) and the empire was at the height of its power.

Making notes on 'The Empire Expands'

This chapter deals with the expansion of the empire under four sultans, three of whom were the greatest warrior (*ghazi*) leaders which the Ottoman empire ever had. You will need to refer to the maps on pages 14, 28 and 38 while making your notes in order to be clear in your mind what happened – and where. It would be a good idea to make a simple time chart of events, in three columns headed the Balkans, the Mediterranean and North Africa, and the East. The following headings and sub-headings should help you to organise your notemaking:

1.   Mehmet the Conqueror
1.1. Europe
       Serbia
       Greece
1.2. Anatolia
2.   Bayezid II
2.1. The Jem affair
2.2. Naval and military achievements
2.3. European politics
2.4. Anatolia
2.5. Assessment of Bayezid II
3.   Selim I
3.1. Anatolia
3.2. Mamluks
3.3. Caliphate
3.4. Europe
3.5. Assessment of Selim I
4.   Suleiman I (the Magnificent)
4.1. The eastern Mediterranean and Rhodes
4.2. The western Mediterranean and North Africa
       Malta
4.3. The Balkans
       Belgrade
       Hungary and Mohaçs
       Vienna
       Hungary again
4.4. The East
       Mamluks
       Persia
       Russia

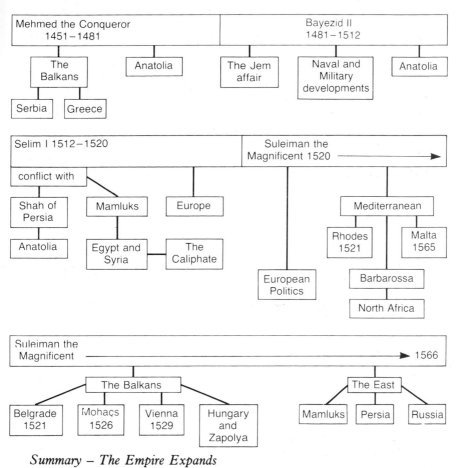

Summary – The Empire Expands

Source-based questions on 'The Empire Expands'

1 Rhodes

Read the extracts on pages 29 and 30. Answer the following questions:

a) In the first extract, explain 'Franks' (line 1). Who were the 'sons of error' (line 1) and the 'sons of the Prophet' (line 10)?

b) In the second extract, what were the 'monstrous piracies' of which Suleiman complained?

c) From the wording of the ultimatum what can be learnt about the Ottoman conventions of war?

d) Western European writers often use the term 'the loss of Rhodes'. In under 200 words write a justification of the conquest of Rhodes from the Ottoman point of view.

CHAPTER 3

Reasons for Ottoman Success 1450–1566: The Sultans

Why did the Ottomans achieve such startling military success in the years between 1450 and 1566? Some of the reasons are internal to the empire. They include the absolute power of the sultan, combined with the personal qualities and abilities of most of those reigning during this period. As one of Ragusa's citizens pointed out to Maximilian I, while western nations were divided among themselves, all supreme authority among the Ottomans rested in a single man. All obeyed the sultan, who alone had complete control of all resources, whether men, materials or money.

The sultan has been called by one historian 'the principal cement of the Ottoman system, the common focus of rulers and ruled alike', master of the Ruling Class, safeguard of the *reaya* (the sultan's 'protected flock'); while another believes that it was 'more as a symbol than as an active and all powerful administrator that the sultan brought together the various elements of Ottoman society'.

Which view is correct? How important was the sultan in fact? And how absolute was he as a ruler?

Prior to the reign of Mehmed the Conqueror, the sultan had simply been the *ghazi* leader, the military commander, nourishing and sustaining Ottoman society by his victories.

1 The *ghaza* raid is our basic duty, as was the case with our fathers. Constantinople, situated as it is in the middle of our dominions, protects the enemies of our state and incites them against us. The conquest of this city is therefore essential to the future and safety
5 of the Ottoman state.

So said Mehmed in 1453 before his conquest of Constantinople made him the most powerful Muslim sultan in the world. He began to see himself as the absolute head of a world-wide empire, heir to the Byzantine and Roman empires, and to think of his new capital, Istanbul, as the centre of the world. A contemporary wrote,

1 In his (the Conqueror's) view, there should be only one empire, only one faith and only one sovereign in the whole world. No place was more deserving than Istanbul for the creation of this unity in the world. The Conqueror believed that, thanks to this
5 city he could extend his rule over the whole world.

To the titles of *Ghazi*, Caesar (Roman emperor), *Basileus* (Greek emperor), Mehmed would have felt entitled to add *Khan*, the title borne by the leader of the steppe tribes from which the Ottomans had come. Within these tribes, tradition dictated that sovereignty was the right and duty of a single family, chosen by God, to bear the burden of government. Among the Ottomans the descendants of Osman ruled without a break (except for the ten year Interregnum after the defeat at Ankara in 1402) until the end of the empire in 1923. The Ottoman state and the Ottoman dynasty were inseparable for over 600 years.

1 The Succession

The succession to the sultanate was not always easy or straightforward. Although it was hereditary within the House of Osman, until the mid-seventeenth century it did not depend on seniority. Before that it was not necessarily the eldest son or senior male relative who became sultan. The choice of the most suitable candidate was believed to lie in the hands of God, and therefore to impose some line of succession would be to oppose the operation of God's will. As Suleiman the Magnificent told one of his own sons, 'You may leave all to God, for it is not man's pleasure but God's will that disposes of kingdoms and their governments. If he has decreed that you shall have the kingdom after me, no living man will be able to prevent it.'

* Quite frequently, however, it was the hand of man and not the will of God which influenced the final choice of sultan. The victory usually went to the eldest son, and more importantly to the son who reached Istanbul first after his father's death, and who had the support of the Janissaries (although believers might say that this *was* the working out of God's will). Mehmed the Conqueror formulated as *kanun* (secular sultanic law) what had previously been merely custom – 'For the welfare of the state, the one of my sons to whom God grants the sultanate may lawfully put his brothers to death.' This Law of Fratricide was intended to give stability to the state by ensuring a single line of succession and preventing civil war among brothers struggling for the throne. During the fifteenth and sixteenth centuries all princes at the age of twelve were despatched to far off parts of the empire as provincial governors. They went there in the care of experienced tutors to learn the business of government. This meant that at the crucial moment of his father's death, the son who was stationed nearest the capital had a considerable advantage. The great officers of state, therefore, often went to extreme lengths to suppress news of the sultan's death until secret messages sent to their candidate for the throne had ensured that he would arrive first in Istanbul and be proclaimed sultan.

When Suleiman the Magnificent died in his tent while on campaign in the Balkans, the Grand Vezir, Sokollu, merely announced that the sultan was suffering from one of his recurrent attacks of gout, and would remain resting in his tent, although he would continue to deal with government business. Every morning Sokollu issued orders as if they came from Suleiman, made new appointments to fill vacancies and gave rewards to those who had distinguished themselves in battle. He sent official messages to other Moslem leaders announcing an Ottoman victory, and sent off the head of the defeated Hungarian leader to the Emperor Maximilian with the sultan's compliments. But the most important message which he sent was to Suleiman's son, Selim, telling him to hurry to Istanbul to claim his inheritance.

Meanwhile Suleiman's body had been secretly embalmed. When the order to return to the capital was given by Sokollu in Suleiman's name, the body was placed in the sultan's carriage. Escorted by guards in exactly the same way as on the outward journey, it seemed as if a living, though sick sultan was leading his victorious troops home. The deception was successfully maintained, until, after three weeks, Sokollu heard that Selim had reached Istanbul. That night the army commanders were informed that Suleiman had died suddenly, and in the morning the army was woken by the chant of prayers for the dead sultan.

*Primogeniture crept in during the seventeenth century, introduced partly on humanitarian grounds to spare unnecessary shedding of blood, and partly because it was thought that the Law of Fratricide had outlived its original purpose of preventing civil war. For a while the sultans continued to send their eldest sons out to the provinces for training in government, while the others were kept in a special part of the royal palace, called the *kafes* (the cage). There they could be easily disposed of if necessary, or kept safely in reserve in case the heir apparent should die. In the later part of the seventeenth century *all* royal princes were kept in the cage. The rooms were small with heavily barred windows and were quite cut off from the rest of the palace. There the princes might be prisoners for 20 or more years or as in the case of Suleiman II for 39 years, during which time they had no contact with anyone apart from their attendants, received no education, were not allowed to marry and lived in constant fear of sudden death. Not surprisingly, by the time the eldest survivor was called to the throne he was a total mental and nervous wreck. Suleiman II sobbed to the messenger who came to bring him the news that he was now sultan, 'If my death had been commanded, say so. Let me perform my prayers, then carry out your orders. Since my childhood, I have suffered nearly forty years of imprisonment. It is better to die at once than to die a little every day'.

In the early years of the empire, the sultan's first official task was to order the execution of any surviving brothers or other male relatives. They were ceremonially strangled with a silken bowstring by deaf mutes who would not be affected by their cries for mercy. Any women of the harem who were pregnant were drowned in case they jeopardised the succession by producing a son. Sometimes, as in 1595, large numbers of family coffins would follow that of the late sultan in the funeral procession. On that particular occasion, not content with disposing of 19 brothers, the sultan had executed 20 or more sisters and 7 step-mothers.

The sultan's second official act was to send formal news of his accession to all the provincial governors in the empire:

1 With God's help I have gained the sultanate . . . as soon as you
  receive this decree proclaim my enthronement to the people in all
  the cities and towns, have my name called at the Friday prayers in
  the mosque (recognition that he and no other was sultan) have
5 cannon fired from the citadels, and festively illuminate the cities
  and towns.

a) The Sultan's Power

Turson Bey, one of the late fifteenth-century Ottoman historians and bureaucrats, wrote about the sultan's power:

1 Without a sovereign, men cannot live in harmony, and may
  perish altogether. God has granted this authority to one person
  only, and that person for the perpetuation of good requires
  absolute obedience.

In theory, although not in practice, the sultan did have absolute power, over the land – all land was the sultan's – over his slaves, over his Moslem subjects (the *reaya*) and over non-Moslems (the *zimmis*) in the Balkans and elsewhere in the empire. He could make laws (*kanuni*) – 'whatever the sultan decrees is law' – but only if he did not contravene religious law (the *sheriat*), which was the basis of the entire Ottoman society. The *sheriat* permeated the whole of life.

The sultan was the secular head of the state, commander-in-chief of the army, head of the government with all government appointments in his gift, chief justice and treasurer. At the same time he was also *imam*, head of the religious institution. In this capacity, he controlled the *ulema* (the whole body of religious personnel, teachers, judges, scribes and scholars), although his actions had to comply with the interpretation of the *sheriat* by the head of the religious institution, the *sheikh-ul-islam*.

If the sultan possessed a strong character, a good intellect, personal courage, administrative ability and, preferably, a certain degree of charm, his authority was unquestioned and his power almost unlimited. If he was weak, incompetent and pleasure loving his position was quickly usurped by officers of state and women of the harem. This was the situation which developed in the seventeenth century.

The Ottoman empire was fortunate in its formative years that, of the first ten sultans, all but one were capable and effective leaders under whose guidance the empire prospered and grew. Of these nine successful sultans, two were outstanding. They are known in the west as Mehmed the Conqueror (1451–1481) and Suleiman the Magnificent (1520–1566). To one of them the empire owed its foundation, to the other its consolidation and expansion. They had much in common – both were great military leaders, strong personalities, able administrators, cultured and intelligent, but ruthless, self-willed and autocratic.

2 Mehmed the Conqueror (1451–1481) (Mehmed Fatih)

Mehmed, the third son of Murad II, was born about 1432. Nothing is known about his mother, apart from the fact that she was probably a Christian-born slave. Even her grave stone does not give her name. In the summer of 1444 at the age of twelve, Mehmed became sultan for the first time, when his father, tired of ceaseless campaigning in the Balkans, decided to abdicate and begin a retirement of pious meditation.

During his first short reign (1444–6) Mehmed was greatly influenced by two men, very different in character and purpose, who did much to shape his ideas and later policies. One was the Grand Vezir, the aristocratic Chandarli Halil Pasha, who as a member of the *ulema* represented the traditions of High Islam. This meant that he favoured a strongly centralised government and a strict religious orthodoxy. He advocated a peaceful policy of co-existence with the empire's Christian neighbours in the Balkans. Nothing, he believed should be done which might alarm the west and provoke an attack, especially while the sultan was so young and unable to lead his army in person as a true *ghazi* should. The other advisor was Zaganos Pasha, one of the slaves of the Porte, who had been Mehmed's tutor and who favoured putting an expansionist policy into immediate effect, with the capture of Constantinople as its first objective. News of this conflict of policies in high places leaked out to the west, where it was seen as an indication of weakness and a signal for an attack on the empire. In the face of this threat, Murad was prevailed upon to return and to take command of the army again.

After winning a great victory against the Christian forces at Varna in November 1444, Murad announced his intention of resuming his interrupted retirement. He was not long left in peace, for a revolt of the Janissaries at Edirne in 1446 recalled him to take control once more. The revolt was probably engineered by Halil Pasha, who knew that it would force Murad to return. Halil Pasha appears to have thought that if there had to be an expansionist policy, it should be under the control of an experienced adult sultan and not under that of a child. The young

Mehmed's first reign was over, but he did not forget who had brought about its end. Five years later he took his revenge.

In 1451 Murad died and Mehmed, now aged 19, found himself sultan again. Western observers of the time wrote him off as weak, inexperienced and likely to prove an ineffective ruler. Few would have believed that 30 years later he would be known as Mehmed the Conqueror (Mehmed Fatih). But Ottoman history is littered with western misconceptions.

Mehmed had been well trained in government through the long established tradition of sending royal princes out to act as provincial governors. He began his reign with four clear, related, political aims: to eliminate Halil Pasha, to ensure the loyalty of Janissaries, thus preventing any further revolt, to make *Jihad* (Holy War) the basis of his foreign policy, and to capture Constantinople.

Constantinople was the key. By its conquest Mehmed would acquire not only the prestige and loyal support resulting from a great military achievement, but also approval for his successful pursuit of Holy War, together with the provision of enormous booty for the victorious army. By Islamic law, a city which refused to surrender became legitimate spoils of war for the sultan and his soldiers who took it by force. By this means the loyalty of the Janissaries would be assured.

The day after the fall of Constantinople, Halil Pasha was arrested. He was subsequently executed. Mehmed chose all but one of his future Grand Vezirs (chief ministers) from among his personal slaves rather than from the old aristocracy or from the *ulema*. No one would again share political power with him. Absolutism was established.

After the fall of Halil Pasha, Mehmed concentrated on the Janissaries. He reorganised and enlarged the corps, and turned it into a well paid, well equipped and highly disciplined force. He developed and increased the use of the *devshirme* slave system to ensure loyalty, both from the army and from his government officers. With this backing, he needed to fear no one, at home or abroad.

a) The Rebuilding of Constantinople

Despite his preoccupation with war for nearly the whole of his reign, Mehmed found time to transform Constantinople into Istanbul, the new capital of the empire. Before the conquest the population had fallen to about 30000. Mehmed began a deliberate programme of repopulation by encouraging refugees to return. He promised them restoration of their property, religious freedom and the opportunity for work. He released the one-fifth share of the prisoners, to which as sultan he was entitled under *sheriat* law, and settled them in the city, and even exempted them from taxation. He ordered 4000 families to be sent from Anatolia and Rumelia and gave them houses which had been deserted. They did not have to be Moslems, but it was expected that they would be merchants, artisans or craftsmen and able to make a contribution to the revival of the city. He also chose Christians from other cities which he had conquered and settled them in different parts of Istanbul. He tried to make the city an ecumenical centre, establishing and protecting Greek Orthodox, Jewish and Armenian communities. To produce food for the new citizens, Mehmed collected 30 000 peasants captured in the Balkans and forcibly settled them in deserted villages outside the walls. Twenty-five years later a census showed Istanbul to have nearly 100 000 inhabitants.

Kritovolous, the Greek chronicler was an eyewitness, and described how Mehmed collected together a number of important and wealthy men from all over the empire and ordered each of them to create an *imaret* in whichever part of the city he wished. An *imaret* was a complex of associated buildings constructed around a mosque, usually including schools and hospitals and all the necessary roads and bridges. Nearby would be commercial buildings, such as inns (caravanserai), mills, markets and bath houses, the income from which would support and maintain the other institutions. *Imarets* were an essential part of all Ottoman towns, and until recently still dominated the skylines of towns and cities all over Anatolia and the Balkans.

After converting the magnificent church of Hagia Sophia (Holy Wisdom) into the great mosque of Aya Sofia, with associated schools, hospitals and libraries, Mehmed completed his *imaret* by building a huge covered market. It had a stone vaulted roof, and iron doors to protect not only the goods of the traders, but the coins and valuables belonging to the city's rich, who used the market as an enormous safe deposit box. Within the market were 12 000 small shops, whose trade supported the mosque complex. This area was to become the business centre not only of Istanbul but also of the whole empire. In the next ten years Mehmed built several other *imarets*, including the largest mosque ever built in the Ottoman empire, all maintained by the income from a series of markets.

New settlers constantly arrived in the capital and the city grew so fast that within 50 years of its conquest it was the largest city in Europe. This huge concentration of population was to have a serious effect on the internal economy of the Ottoman empire in the seventeenth century. Mehmed arranged for repairs to the walls for the defence of the city, and to the aqueducts which provided the city's water supply. He often personally supervised and inspected the work which he had ordered to be done on the roads, bridges and public buildings, and himself drew up plans for a palace in the centre of the city. This palace, afterwards known as Eski Saray (the old palace), proved unsatisfactory, and in 1464 Topkapi Saray (the new palace) was built nearer the shores of the Bosphorus.

The Ottomans were justly proud of their new and beautiful city, and it was frequently celebrated by court poets:

1 We have not seen its peer in any land
  It has none, save perhaps in Paradise.
  There is no land or city that is like it
  No place to live that can compare with it.
5
  Stamboul, thou peerless of cities, thou jewel beyond compare
  Seated astride upon two seas, with dazzling light aflare!
  Resplendent as the sun whose rays the world in light enshrine
10 Thy gardens visions of delight, patterns of joy divine.
  (Stamboul was an alternative name for Istanbul.)

Unfortunately, all this work on Istanbul, as well as the almost incessant warfare, put a strain on national resources. Several times Mehmed was forced to devalue the coinage. He issued new coins which contained only five-sixths as much silver as the old ones for which they were exchanged. This meant that people lost one-fifth of the value of the money they had. The government had gained at their expense. Mehmed raised money by other equally unpopular means. He established government monopolies on the sale of such necessities as candlewax, salt and soap, and farmed out these monopolies to individuals, who made their profit by charging very high prices for the goods. Worse still in public estimation was Mehmed's action over the *vakif* (pious foundation). This was an Islamic arrangement by which owners of income-producing properties assigned them in perpetuity to provide for public charitable or religious institutions, such as roads and bridges, hospitals, schools and mosques. Mehmed took the view that since all land had originally belonged to the sultan, if it had been turned into private property and made *vakif* it had been done so illegally. He therefore simply confiscated it and redistributed it as new *timars*. This had the result of increasing the number of *sipahis* available for the army, but it also upset the vested interests of many wealthy and influential families who had set up *vakifs* as family foundations from which they obtained financial benefits. By taking control of the *vakif* lands, Mehmed considered that he was merely reverting to traditional practice, while at the same time centralising political power in his own hands.

b) Mehmed the Man

One of the very few contemporary descriptions of Mehmed is that by Gian-Maria Angiello, written in 1481, the last year of Mehmed's life:

1 Known as the Grand Turk, he was of medium height, fat and
  fleshy; he had a wide forehead, large eyes with thick lashes, an
  aquiline nose, a small mouth, a round full reddish-tinged beard, a

short thick neck and a loud voice. He suffered from gout in the
5 legs.

We also have a portrait by Gentile Bellini which is now known not to be
an accurate representation, although Bellini was working at the Ottoman court about 1480, when the portrait was painted. It is in poor
condition and seems to have been over painted at some time. In fact
X-ray investigations appear to show that only the turban is original!

Mehmed was an open-minded cultured man who brought Bellini
from Venice to decorate his palace walls with Italian-style frescoes.
Italian authors flocked to offer him their works on geography and
military tactics, and to praise him in classical Latin poems. He filled a
library with Greek and Latin manuscripts, and showed his interest in
lands outside the empire by ordering a map of the world, and a
translation of Ptolemy's *Geography*. He gathered scholars from Italy,
Greece and Trebizond around him, and commissioned a history of the
Roman empire. He arranged for the Greek Patriarch to prepare an
instruction manual on Christianity for him. Under his personal patron-
age, Ottoman scholars made real advances in the study of mathematics,
astronomy and medicine, and the teaching of these subjects along with
logic and theology, became part of the standard educational curriculum
of the *ulema*. Mehmed himself reopened a longstanding controversy
over the relationship between philosophy and religion, and invited two
of the outstanding theologians of the day to debate the matter in a series
of written exchanges, to be judged by the *ulema*.

Western historians have frequently claimed that Mehmed was a
Renaissance monarch. They base this assertion on his contacts with the
west, his wide ranging intellectual and artistic interests, his involvement in the rebuilding and beautification of Istanbul and his views on
sovereignty. Turkish historians would not agree with this view. For
them he was culturally a Moslem, devoted to his faith and following the
spiritual guidance of the *sheikh-ul-islam*. Members of the *ulema* came
several days a week to the palace to debate with him and to give him
religious instruction. His only interest in the Christian world was that
of a man who wanted to know what to expect when he attacked and
conquered it. By understanding the west, he believed he would be able
to rule it.

In May, 1451, Mehmed died at the age of 49, soon after setting out
from Istanbul on a new campaign against eastern Anatolia. The cause of
his death is unknown, and rumours that he was poisoned, still
sometimes purveyed by western authors as fact, are quite unsubstanti-
ated.

c) Assessment

Estimates of Mehmed's personality, as a ruler and as a man, vary widely. To the contemporary westerner, he was the destroyer, the arch-enemy of Christianity, and there was great rejoicing when the news of his death reached Venice. Stories of his violence and cruelty are often repeated, but they are derived almost entirely from unreliable contemporary or near contemporary sources. He was probably no worse, if no better, than any other absolute ruler of his times.

To the Turks Mehmed has always been *Fatih*, the Conqueror. Some would say that he was the greatest of the sultans, unparalleled in the history of the world, who shone even brighter than his great-grandson, Suleiman the Magnificent. Mehmed was a warrior who strove for world domination, and who was at the same time both a man of tolerance and culture and a harsh ruler, who never forgot that he was an Islamic *ghazi* sovereign, whose mission was Holy War. He was the true founder of the Ottoman empire.

3 Suleiman the Magnificent (1520–1566)

The long reign of Suleiman I, called Suleiman the Magnificent in the west, but *Kanuni* (the law giver) by the Turks, has traditionally been regarded, in both east and west, as the high point of Ottoman achievement.

Almost all that is known of Suleiman's early life is that he was born about 1494 in the old Greek city of Trebizond on the Black Sea coast of Anatolia, where he lived until he was about 15. He was the only surviving son of Selim I, and his accession was unusual in that it was unchallenged.

As in the case of Mehmed the Conqueror, there were gloomy forecasts about Suleiman's prospects and abilities, but, like Mehmed, he was to prove his critics wrong. His reign was a series of military triumphs abroad, and administrative and legal achievements at home.

a) Suleiman the Man

There are a number of western portraits of Suleiman, some very fanciful. The best likeness is probably that in the engraving by Melchior Lorchs, 1559 (see page 55). No sultan ever sat for a western painter, but comparison with a known portrait of an Ottoman artist, probably painted from life, shows the Lorchs engraving to be a good likeness. Lorchs is thought to have based his portrait on a painting given to de Busbeq, in whose entourage he was employed.

Other evidence for Suleiman's appearance can be found in contemporary eyewitness descriptions. At the beginning of his reign a Venetian observer wrote:

1 He is twenty-five years of age and of a delicate complexion. His
  neck is a little too long, his face thin, his nose aquiline. He has a

light moustache and a small beard; he has a pleasant expression,
though his skin tends to pallor. He is said to be a wise lord, fond
5 of study, and men hope for good from his rule.

When de Busbecq first arrived in Istanbul he gave his impressions of
Suleiman:

1 He is beginning to feel the weight of his years, but his dignity of
  demeanour and his general physical appearance are worthy of the
  ruler of so vast an empire. He has always been frugal and
  temperate and was so even in his youth ... Even his bitterest
5 critics can find nothing more serious to allege against him than his
  undue submission to his wife ... He is a strict guardian of his
  religion and its ceremonies, being not less desirous of upholding
  his faith than of extending his dominions. For his age – he is
10 almost sixty – he enjoys quite good health, though his bad
  complexion may be due to some hidden malady ...

In the last year of the Sultan's reign, 1566, a Venetian *bailo*
(representative) wrote:

1 He is very feeble of body, so that he lacks little of dying, being
  dropsical, with swollen legs, appetite gone, face swelled and of a
  very bad colour. In March he had four or five fainting fits, and has
  had one since, in which his attendants doubted whether he was
5 alive or dead.

De Busbeq, about the same time, also commented on Suleiman's poor
health:

1 It may be that his bad complexion arises from some lurking
  malady. There is a notion current that he has an incurable ulcer or
  cancer on his thigh. When he is anxious to impress an ambassador
  ... he conceals the bad complexion of his face under a coat of
5 rouge ... for he fancies that it contributes to inspire greater fear
  in foreign potentates if they think he is well and strong.

In passing, de Busbeq gives many small interesting snippets of
information about Suleiman. He tells, for instance, that Suleiman
always wore robes of mohair, and favoured the colour green, said to
have been the favourite colour of the Prophet Mohammed.

But these are superficial descriptions of the Sultan's external appearance and behaviour. What can we learn about the man himself, his
character and personality? There are a number of clues. Suleiman's
reign is well documented, beginning with his own journal, kept
throughout his life and particularly while he was on campaign. Rather

Portrait of Suleiman engraved by Melchior Lorchs, 1559

strangely he always refers to himself in the third person, and the majority of the entries are, to say the least, brief and matter of fact. This in itself is illuminating. All his life, Suleiman was remarkable for the lack of emotion which he showed, even at the most dramatic moments. The reason for this is not easy to determine, for no hard evidence is available. In his campaign diaries he often combines in a single sentence the horrors around him and everyday events. This gives to many of the entries a feeling of chilling unreality. During the 1521 Hungarian campaign he wrote:

1 7th July. News came of the capture of Sabaç; a hundred heads of soldiers of garrison who had been unable to escape were brought

to camp. The next day these heads were stuck on pikes along the roadside and Ahmed Pasha came to kiss hands.

5 2nd August. Attack on Belgrade. Assault; moat is filled up with corpses; five or six hundred men are lost.

After the battle of Mohaçs in 1526:

1 31st August. The sultan seated on a golden throne receives homage of *vezirs* and *beys*; massacre of 2000 prisoners; rain falls in torrents.

1st September. Rest at Mohaçs; 20 000 Hungarian infantry and 5 4000 cavalry buried.

It is known that he and his beloved wife Roxelana carried on a lengthy correspondence when he was away from Istanbul, but only a few of her letters, and none of his, have survived. The tone of her letters, most of them written in her own hand, is affectionate. They are full of family detail, her concern for his gout, the treatment needed for their hunchback son Jehangir, news of the plague in the capital, mysterious references to a talismanic shirt, inscribed with holy names, which will turn away bullets, and on one occasion an entertaining story of how she drank a bottle of eau-de-cologne by mistake. It is a pity we do not have any of Suleiman's replies; they might cast rather a different light on his character. As it is we have to make do with his poetry, written under his pen name, *Muhibbi*, the affectionate one, to find any evidence of his emotions. Otherwise he appears cold, hard and unfeeling.

Some of Suleiman's most distressing moments were due to problems within his own family, but even then he betrayed absolutely no emotion. In accordance with eastern custom, the Ottoman sultans maintained a harem of slaves, most of them Christian-born women from the Balkans. Only a few of these became the sultan's wives, and then only if they bore sons, while others remained as concubines. (No legal difference was made between their children and those of the wives. Status of the children depended only on order of birth.) The majority of the harem were married off at the age of 25 to pages in the palace service. Suleiman's first wife was the mother of his eldest son, Mustafa, while his second, favourite and very influential wife, known as Roxelana (the Russian woman) in the west, and as Hurrem (the laughing one) to the Ottomans, was the mother of four more sons. The rivalry of these two women on behalf of their sons led to the murder of two of those sons, and indirectly to the death of a third.

Roxelana, fairhaired, intelligent and charming was the first of the harem women to play a prominent part in state affairs. In the seventeenth century the influence of the harem became commonplace in Ottoman politics. Roxelana built up a 'harem party', with the help of the French ambassador – the first time that a foreign ambassador is known to have played any part in Ottoman internal affairs. This party influenced Suleiman, first against the Grand Vezir Ibrahim, and then against the Sultan's popular eldest son and probable successor, Mustafa. Through her son-in-law, Rustem Pasha, now the Grand Vezir, Roxelana seems to have started rumours that Mustafa, with the help of the Janissaries, was planning an armed rebellion against his father. A forged letter persuaded Suleiman to take action.

De Busbecq gives a graphic account of events when Mustafa was summoned to his father's campaign tent at Karaman in September, 1553:

1 Everything appeared peaceful – there were no soldiers or attendants to inspire fear of treachery. However, several mutes, strong
  sturdy men were there, and as soon as he entered the tent, they
  tried to throw a noose around him. Being a man of powerful
5 build, he defended himself strongly, and fought not only for
  himself but for the throne, for there was no doubt that if he could
  escape and throw himself upon the Janissaries outside, they
  would not only protect him but proclaim him sultan. Suleiman,
10 fearing this, and being separated only by the linen tent hangings
  from the scene, and finding there was a delay in the execution of
  his plan, thrust his head out and directed fierce and threatening
  glances at the mutes, and by menacing gestures rebuked their
15 hesitation. The mutes redoubled their efforts, hurled Mustafa to
  the ground, and, throwing the bowstring round his neck, strangled him. They then laid the corpse on a rug in front of the tent.
  When the news spread through the camp, pity and grief were
20 general throughout the army.

The death of Mustafa was seen by contemporaries as a blot on Suleiman's reputation. The Janissaries, the *ulema* and the bureaucracy agreed, however, that the true culprits were Roxelana and Rustem Pasha. Each year was identified by a descriptive phrase, a chrongram, and that given to 1553 was 'the wiles of Rustem Pasha'. Most unusually on the death of a prince, a flood of lament was published and circulated in the next few years, which while attacking Suleiman, left no doubt that others were to blame:

1 O king of noble blood, is this justice?
  You may be lord of the world, but is this proper government?
  Is this tenderness to kill someone as dear to you as Mustafa?
  You killed him by a lying trick and where is the truth in that?
5 You have been deluded by the words of an enemy; is that love?
  You have shed his blood, is that the justice of a caliph?
  What's become of Mustafa? Why did you kill him, my sultan?

God save us! The world is falling about our ears.
10 The sun of beauty of the house of Osman has set, its counsels lie
in disorder, and by a trick its honour has been besmirched. The
devil's work has caused the passing of this man worth many men.

In fairness to Suleiman however, it must be said that there is some
evidence that Mustafa had been plotting against his father for ten years
past. At the time of Mustafa's murder, Suleiman was quite seriously ill.
He may genuinely have feared that his eldest son, so popular with the
Janissaries, was about to take advantage of the situation and to seize the
throne.

Soon after Mustafa's murder, Suleiman's hunchback son died, it was
said, of grief. Of the remaining sons, Mehmed, the originally intended
heir had died young, while Bayezid and Selim, concerned for the
succession, were only kept from open warfare by the efforts of their
mother, Roxelana. When she died in 1558, Suleiman separated them
sending them as governors of provinces far apart, in the hope of
preserving peace between them. This did not happen, and when in
1561 civil war broke out between them, Suleiman who favoured Selim,
ordered the execution of Bayezid. Bayezid entreated his father for
mercy in true Ottoman style, by sending him a lengthy poem, with the
refrain 'Father, my illustrious sultan, I am guiltless, God knows.' The
pleas went unheeded. Bayezid sought sanctuary with the Shah of
Persia, who welcomed him warmly and then betrayed him to Suleiman
for money (although he in fact actually received very little of it). An
emissary was sent and Bayezid and his five sons were strangled. Selim
had become his father's sole heir.

If Suleiman showed no sorrow at the deaths he himself had ordered
of his friend Ibrahim (see page 79), and of his sons Mustafa and
Bayezid, he equally showed no pleasure at the unexpected naval victory
at Djerba in 1560. The indefatigable de Busbecq writes:

1 Those who saw Suleiman's face in the hour of triumph, failed to
detect in it the slightest trace of undue elation. I can myself
positively declare that when I saw him two days later on his way
to the mosque the expression of his countenance was unchanged;
5 his stern features had lost nothing of their habitual gloom; one
would have thought that the victory concerned him not, and that
this startling success of arms caused him no surprise. So self-
contained was the heart of the grand old man, so schooled to meet
10 each change of fortune, however great, that all the applause and
triumph of that day wrung from him no sign of satisfaction.

Although Suleiman always emphasised the importance which he
attached to his position as Caliph, the 'Protector of the Holy Cities' (of
Mecca and Medina) and therefore the most important of the Moslem

rulers of his day, he seems never to have made the pilgrimage to Mecca. This is thought to have been because he intensely disliked the idea of going to sea, and is known never to have even set foot on a ship. For this reason, he was content to leave the conduct of naval affairs in the Mediterranean to Barbarossa and Dragut. He personally spent 10 years in the field, commanding 13 major campaigns in the Balkans and Persia. But it was more than military success which gave splendour to his reign. Equally important were his domestic achievements.

b) Suleiman the Lawgiver

He introduced a legal system designed to protect the lives, property and honour of all individuals, irrespective of religion. For example, soldiers while on the march were not to live off the land, to the great detriment of the local peasantry, but were to pay for their food; taxes were to be levied according to ability to pay and government officials were to be appointed only on merit and to be dismissed only for good reason. Laws such as these formalised what was supposed to be, but was not always, existing practice.

All this legal work brought large numbers of lawyers into the Sultan's service, and their supervision was entrusted to the current Grand Vezir, Lufti Pasha. He was a remarkable man – poet, jurist, soldier and administrator – who between 1539 and 1541 began to collect together customary laws and administrative practices from various parts of the empire. These were incorporated into a new law code (*kanun-nahme*) issued in Suleiman's name. These sultanic laws (*kanuns*) were concerned with justice and finance. They laid down penalties for robbery, drunkenness and similar crimes.

The same law code also contained detailed regulations for the conduct of *timar* holders, a new range of taxes on animals and other items, and severe penalties for attempting to evade payment of customs duties. Illegal taxes, imprisonment without trial and confiscation of property without compensation were all prohibited. A new departure was the laying down of acceptable levels of taxation. For the first time the government accepted that the *reaya* could not be expected to pay ever heavier taxes, and that state spending on the army would have to be cut if the budget was to be balanced.

For the five years between 1543 and 1548 Suleiman was not on campaign. During this time in Istanbul he concentrated much of his attention on further legal reforms. He enforced regulations to ensure that only able and learned men would be admitted to the *ulema*, and that they would serve honestly and efficiently. High standards were required of all courts of law, although Suleiman's insistence that the judges' authority came as much from sultanic as from religious law was, later in the seventeenth century, to give an unscrupulous sultan the chance to demand that the courts must always follow his wishes.

These years saw the promulgation of yet another law code, 'The Law Code of the House of Osman', which made further detailed regulations in various areas, but, most importantly, legalised the making of *vakif* grants which Mehmed the Conqueror had abolished. All newly conquered lands were to be *miri* lands (state owned), but a concession allowed individuals living there to have rights of ownership over their house, garden and small movable objects. They could buy and sell these things and leave them to their heirs.

With all this welter of legislation issued in his name and, perhaps, although there is no certainty of this, at his instigation, it is not surprising that Suleiman was known as *kanuni*, the law giver. The volume of law enacted during his reign was far greater than that of any other sultan before or after. Contemporaries spoke of his zeal for justice, and certainly his reign was notable for the emergence of a number of extremely able jurists, whose reputation spread far beyond the frontiers of the empire.

c) Suleiman's Magnificence

However, all was not entirely well. By the end of his reign rises in population, food shortages and inflation were beginning to be felt, foreshadowing the problems of the next century (see page 125). Some of these problems, rises in population for instance, were general throughout most of Europe, but Suleiman and his government may have been directly responsible for some of the economic difficulties which arose within the empire after 1550. The expenses of a vast new bureaucracy, almost continuous war and the splendours of the court and palace all contributed to the pressure on the Ottoman economy. Perhaps magnificence was bought at too high a price.

It was of course the splendours of his court and the brilliance of his military victories which so impressed foreign visitors and earned Suleiman the title of Magnificent. Of his personal magnificence there is no doubt. His jewellery and robes were superb; enthroned on cushions of gold, he is described in 1544, as dressed in a gown of white satin, with a medium sized turban over a bonnet of pleated crimson velvet. On the turban was a gold rosette, set with a cut ruby the size of a hazelnut, and in his right ear a pear shaped pearl of the same size; this was on an ordinary court occasion. During the elaborate ceremonies staged for the festivities attending the circumcision of the royal princes in 1530, the delights and splendours far outweighed anything dreamt of at the Field of the Cloth of Gold, where Francis I of France met Henry VIII of England, or at the great Venetian and Florentine spectaculars. The firework displays alone were breathtaking. Animals moved round the arena with rockets strapped to their backs, and there were fire-breathing serpents and splendid set-pieces of windmills and galleys silhouetted against the sky.

The Byzantine court ceremonial which had been taken over by Mehmed the Conqueror after the capture of Constantinople, was formalised under Suleiman. The colour, shape and size of turbans became a matter of law. Every man took his exact social place in the court assemblies (no women were present), every man knew and observed meticulously his rank and exacted his precise title. The weekly processions to the mosque for Friday prayers were an unrivalled opportunity for sorting out orders of precedence. While previously it had been a time when anyone could approach the sultan and by touching his robe gain the right to present a petition, now no one might approach the sultan too closely, let alone touch his person.

A Venetian who saw the procession in the early 1560s described how:

1 when in Istanbul the sultan goes to one of three mosques. With him go 40 or 50 mace-bearers on horseback. They are followed by perhaps 2000 Janissaries on foot, with swords, axes at their girdles and guns with barrels five palms long at their backs; and
5 by the same number of sipahis on horseback, with swords, bows and arrows and maces at their saddlebows. All march in silence, nothing being heard but the sound of their feet and the trampling of the horses. Then come 15 or 20 led horses, all with rich
10 head-trappings adorned with carbuncles, diamonds, sapphires, turquoises and great pearls, the saddles not being seen because they are covered with housings of scarlet velvet. Near the Great Turk himself no one rides, but four grooms walking on either side
15 of him, about a pike's length off, to keep the people away. Before him always go three pages, one carrying his bow and arrows, another his sabre and the third a bottle of scented water to wash with at the door of the mosque.

Behind him also rode two pages with a cushion for the sultan to sit on in the mosque.

Protocol and precedence had become all important. Western Europe was to see nothing like it, until the Versailles of Louis XIV's equally absolutist France.

Even on military campaigns formality prevailed. In his tent

1 the sultan was seated on a very low couch, not a foot from the ground, which was covered in costly rugs and cushions of exquisite workmanship. Near him lay his bows and arrows . . . on entering we were separately conducted into the royal presence by
5 the chamberlains, who grasped our arms [this was because of an attempt by a visitor to assassinate an earlier sultan during an audience] and after a pretence of kissing his hand, we were conducted backwards to the wall opposite his seat, care being
10 taken that we should never turn out backs upon him. All around

was glittering with gold, silver and purple; with silk and with velvet; it was the most beautiful thing I ever saw.

De Busbecq reports too how dispatches were wrapped in cloth of gold and how he was given robes of silk, heavily embroidered 'as many as I could carry'.

Under Suleiman however, the sultan's magnificence was not simply a personal matter of his dress or his jewels, or even of the formalised court rituals. It had become an integral part of the Ottoman state itself. The contemporary Ottoman account, by one of his senior officials, describes Suleiman's ceremonial departure from Edirne at the start of his Hungarian campaign in 1543. It was a scene of splendour on a grand scale – not just a procession to impress his subjects, although no doubt it did that too, but a means to dazzle, astound and intimidate the enemy. It was not just the sultan riding to war, but the whole glorious might of the Ottoman empire marching with him. After the baggage train of 8000 camels, mules and horses came an advance corps of 3000 gunners with their equipment, followed by all the palace officials and their staff, their personal slaves and servants. Surrounded by banners and pennants rode the cavalry in groups of 2000, together with officials of the *Divan*, closely followed by the Sultan's hounds, horses and falcons. 12000 Janissaries marched immediately before the Sultan, accompanied by 100 trumpeters and 100 drummers. Around Suleiman himself were 400 mounted bodyguards (the Sipahis of the Porte), and hundreds of pursuivants, carrying silver staves, and richly dressed in silks and cloth of gold, and all shouting and cheering as the Sultan rode in their midst.

While the court ceremonials were formal, sumptuous and designed to enhance his position as absolute ruler by placing him above common mortals, there is no doubt that Suleiman was himself an extremely cultured and learned man. He was a scholar, poet and goldsmith, for in the princely tradition of the time he had been trained in a craft. He was a discerning collector of precious and beautiful objects which came his way in the course of his campaigns, and acquired many more through the luxury trades which developed during his reign and largely through his interest. He beautified and extended the Topkapi Palace, and built the great Suleimanyie complex of mosque, schools, hospitals and other public buildings on the site of Mehmed the Conqueror's old palace (Eski Saray). Under the guidance of his friend, the famous architect, Sinan, he built mosques, bridges and roads in cities throughout the empire. At his court men of ability gathered. Poets and scholars, who wrote on logic, theology and grammar, compiled biographies of the 600 most important learned men of the fifteenth century, and produced a history of the House of Osman from the beginning to the death of Selim I. A substantial quantity of Suleiman's own poetry has survived. It was written both in Ottoman and in Persian, and 12 lengthy manuscripts of lyric poetry have now been identified as his.

d) Assessment

When Suleiman died after a reign of nearly 50 years, he left a great sense of loss. The poet Baki expressed it poignantly:

1 Will not the king wake from sleep? Broke has the dawn of day.
Will he not move forth from his tent bright as heaven's display?
Long have our eyes dwelt on the road, and yet no news has come
From yonder land . . .

Yet it must be asked whether his reputation is justified. Without the efforts of his father, Selim I (the most underrated of all the sultans) could Suleiman have achieved as much as he did? Suleiman's military conquests and his legal achievements were all built on the back of his father's work. Selim's conquests of Egypt and Syria, and his defeat of the Persians secured the eastern borders of the empire and made it possible for Suleiman to embark on a *ghazi* career in the Balkans and Mediterranean without fear of being attacked from the rear. Selim's capture of the Holy Cities of Mecca and Medina paved the way for Suleiman to become Protector of Islam, and the most important Moslem ruler. Selim's legal codes were the basis of Suleiman's early *kanuns* and the pattern for his later ones.

For Europeans, then and now, Suleiman was, above all, the successful military leader. In that lay his greatness. His magnificence was something extra, and came from the splendours of his life style. For the contemporary Ottoman, as for the modern Turk, the view of Suleiman's reign as the Golden Age derives partly from the fact that it was the last time that Ottoman armies were able to meet those of the Christians on equal terms. But just as important were domestic achievements. Not only was Suleiman the law maker, he was also the good administrator. Under him the Ottoman state system worked. The *devshirme* and the *timar* systems functioned well, and the Circle of Equity (see page 117) was maintained. The very length of the reign created an impression of political and economic stability, while the feeling of awe in which the Sultan was held was increased by the formalised and impersonal rituals of the magnificent court.

Suleiman seemed to his contemporaries, at home and abroad, a figure larger than life. Is it because he is now seen, nostalgically, against a background of known later decline, that he is still such a figure? Or is the verdict justified?

Making notes on '*Reasons for Ottoman Success: The Sultans***'***

There were many reasons for Ottoman success in the fifteenth and sixteenth centuries. This chapter is concerned with only one of them, the importance of the sultan. It discusses first the sultanate in general, and how far the sultan's power was absolute, and then goes on to look in detail at two sultans in particular, Mehmed the Conqueror and Suleiman the Magnificent. Bearing in mind the information which you already have from the previous chapter about their military achievements, try to decide, as you make your notes from the following headings and sub-headings, whether their reputations are justified.

1   The sultans
1.1. The succession
      Law of Fratricide
      Primogeniture
1.2. The sultan's power
2.   Mehmed the Conqueror
2.1. Rebuilding of Constantinople
2.2. Mehmed the man
2.3. Assessment of Mehmed the Conqueror
3.   Suleiman the Magnificent
3.1. Suleiman the man
3.2. Suleiman the Lawgiver
3.3. Suleiman's magnificence
3.4. Assessment of Suleiman

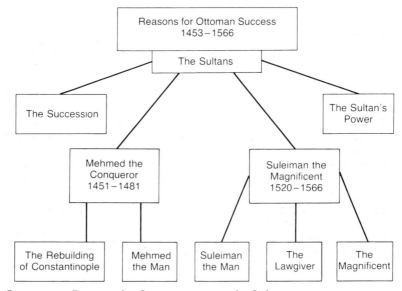

Summary – Reasons for Ottoman success: the Sultans

Source based questions on 'Reasons for Ottoman Success: The Sultans'

1 Constantinople

Read the two short extracts on page 44, and look at the plan on page 64. Answer the following questions.

a) In the first extract, explain *ghaza*. Why was it 'our basic duty'?

b) How do the two extracts differ in their explanation of Mehmed's motives for the conquest of Constantinople? What were in fact his motives?

2 Suleiman the Magnificent

Read the four descriptions of Suleiman given on pages 53–54, and examine the portrait on page 55. Answer the following questions:

a) What can be learnt from the first extract about its author's expectations of a good ruler?

b) Explain the significance of the phrase 'his undue submission to his wife' in the second extract.

c) How accurate is the opinion expressed by de Busbecq in the second extract that Suleiman was 'not less desirous of upholding his faith than of extending his dominions'?

d) What impression of Suleiman is the artist attempting to present? Explain your answer so as to identify the techniques used by the artist. Does the portrait accord with the written descriptions?

e) What are de Busbecq's feelings towards Suleiman? Base your answer on evidence contained in the second and fourth extracts.

3 The Death of Mustafa, 1553

Read the description of Mustafa's death on page 57 and the extracts from the two laments on pages 57–58. Answer the following questions:

a) In the first passage, describe Suleiman's likely motive for using 'mutes' to strangle Mustafa.

b) In the first lament, explain the phrases 'by a lying trick' (line 4), and 'the justice of a caliph' (line 6), and in the second lament, explain, 'the house of Osman' (line 10).

c) What impressions of Mustafa are given by these passages? Are the impressions 'complementary' or 'contradictory'? Explain your answer.

d) What significance does the author of the second lament see in the death of Mustafa?

e) De Busbecq was not an eyewitness of Mustafa's death. How reliable is his account likely to be? Explain your answer.

CHAPTER 4

Reasons for Ottoman Success 1450–1566: The Organisation of the State

The absolute authority and power of able and effective sultans gave the Ottoman state unity and stability in the years between 1450 and 1566. But this would not have been possible without the highly organised military, administrative and economic system operating within the empire during this period.

1 The Devshirme

Originally the needs of the Ottoman state for slaves was met by prisoners of war. When the supply of these proved insufficient, the *devshirme* was introduced, some time before 1395.

The *devshirme* (literally 'the gathering') was the collection of a tax in the form of boys from Christian peasant families in the Balkans for the sultan's service. The size and frequency of the collection depended on the particular needs of the government at the time – heavy losses among the Janissaries as the result of fierce campaigning, for instance, meant that many new recruits were needed. Before a 'gathering' took place, each village or group of villages in the chosen area was designated a 'tax-unit'. This was assessed to provide a given number of boys, who had to be strong and healthy, and, in the sixteenth century, aged between 8 and 18. In the early seventeenth century the age limits appear to have been 15 to 20. Boys who were orphans, only sons, already married, sickly, skilled tradesmen or had 'behavioural problems' were exempt. It used to be thought that all other boys of the correct age within the collecting area were automatically taken, but it now seems that this was not so. In fact, because of the assessment system, only about one family in 40 had to provide a boy on any particular occasion.

When a *devshirme* was ordered, Janissary officers took the sultan's written authorisation to the *sanjaks* involved. They stopped in large towns, informed the local *cadis* and the *timar*-holders of the area, and sent messages to the outlying villages instructing fathers to bring their sons for inspection. Local priests were ordered to bring in the baptismal records, so that details of the boys' age, parentage and place of residence could be noted down in a register. A careful description of each boy was also made, to prevent possible substitutions.

Between 1000 and 3000 boys were collected at any one time. They were sorted into groups of 100 or so, dressed in special and distinctive clothes, and sent under Jannissary escort to Istanbul. The western view of this is embodied in the words of de Busbecq, the Imperial ambassador to Suleiman the Magnificent:

1 I met various gangs of wretched Christian slaves of every kind who were being led to horrible servitude . . . driven along in herds, or else were tied together with chains and driven along in a line. I could scarcely restrain my tears in pity for their plight.

The Ottomans would not have accepted this view. They regarded the *devshirme* simply as payment of a tax, not the enslavement of their own subjects. Although the boys lost their personal freedom, and usually lost touch with their families and homes, they received an excellent education and training and their career prospects were far above anything they could have dreamed of in their native villages.   As a Venetian *bailo* (representative) in Istanbul wrote to his government,

1 It is a fact truly worth much consideration that the riches, the force of government, in short the whole state of the Ottoman empire, is founded upon and placed in the hands of persons all born in the faith of Christ, who are made slaves and transferred
5 into the Mohammedan sect.

In due course, Moslem families sometimes tried to buy a place in the tribute for their sons, so attractive was the future for the *devshirme* boys. Moslem boys were excluded because, according to one Ottoman writer:

1 If they were to become slaves of the Sultan they would abuse the privilege. Their relatives would oppress the *reaya* and not pay taxes. They would become rebels. But Christian children accept Islam and become enemies of their relatives.

In the seventeenth century, when the *devshirme* came to an end, events proved the point. The whole ethos of the Ottoman administrative system changed, when free-born Moslems replaced the ex-Christian slaves. To a large extent, as the writer had feared, self-interest replaced dedicated service. In addition there was a lowering of quality among the bureaucracy staff caused by a decline in the standard of training and education which they received. These factors, combined with the sultans' loss of authority, reduced central government's control over the provinces, and disturbed the Circle of Equity (see page 117).

*When the *devshirme* boys arrived in Istanbul, the best, probably about 10%, were selected for service in the sultan's palace, where they received special training. They had to be handsome, physically fit and intelligent. At any one time there would be about 700 pages in various stages of training. Some of them would eventually become the sultan's personal attendants, of whom there were never more than 39. This was the highest rank it was possible to achieve within the palace, for, as in all eastern countries, importance was determined by physical closeness to the person of the sovereign. Most of the pages would leave the Inner Service (within the palace) for the Outer Service, and either take up positions in provincial government, or become *Sipahis* of the *Porte*, the sultan's mounted bodyguard.

Before that, all pages followed a long and arduous training. They were first converted to Islam, circumcised and taught the rudiments of the faith. Along with this, they 'are set to learning the alphabet. There are four teachers; one drills the boys in reading, another teaches the Koran in Arabic, a third teaches Persian, while a fourth teaches Arabic literature.' Later they learnt law, and how to interpret judges' reports. Rewards for progress were given in the form of pay awards. They received 'scarlet garments twice a year, and robes of white cloth for summer.' Contemporary drawings show the pages dressed in long dark robes and wearing tall white pointed caps, like dunces' caps. Like the women of the harem, the pages were under the supervision of eunuchs, slaves who had been castrated. Discipline was severe, although not, by the standards of the time, considered excessively so. Punishment did not normally exceed being beaten on the soles of the feet once a day, and with not more than ten strokes on any one occasion. The pages lived a restricted life, conducted according to a strict timetable, with little freedom to converse and no chance to leave the palace. Their only recreation was sport, and they were expected to become expert horsemen and proficient in fencing, archery and wrestling. Each was also expected to learn a craft.

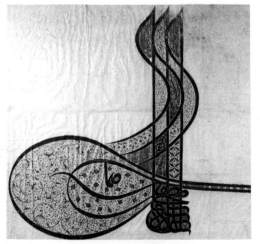

An example of Ottoman calligraphic art: the Tugra, *the Sultan's monogram used to authenticate official documents*

After a period of between two and seven years, depending on their age at entry into the palace, the pages underwent another selection test. The most able continued to move up through the Palace Chambers (schools), while the remainder left to join the sultan's cavalry. The future of those who stayed within the palace was carefully considered, and according to their temperaments, each boy was prepared for a career, usually in government service.

Palace education aimed to produce 'the warrior statesman and loyal Moslem, who at the same time should be a man of letters and polished speech, profound courtesy and honest morals.' But the basic aim, although not always openly admitted, was to inculcate complete obedience and loyalty to the sultan. The boys were taught that the greatest blessing they could receive would be death in the sultan's service. The system provided a totally loyal body of highly educated professional men, with no family ties. Despite their slave status they enjoyed great wealth and power as members of the Ottoman ruling class, with no interests but those of the sultan. When the pages left the palace at the age of twenty-five they received the sultan's personal blessing, an embroidered coat and a horse. They formed the backbone of the Ottoman local and central administrative system, giving the Empire a civil service more efficient than any in western Europe. This was the second strength of the Empire.

2 The Janissaries

Those of the *devshirme* boys who were not considered suitable for palace service, generally became Janissaries (*Yenicheri*, new troops). The Janissaries are said to have been formed originally from the sultan's share of the prisoners of war taken at the capture of Adrianople in 1369, and had become the basis of the Ottoman standing army.

Mehmed the Conqueror, after suppressing a revolt of the Janissaries early in his reign, had reformed the corps, improved their pay and modernised their equipment. At the same time he had greatly increased their numbers to around 10000, a large number for a standing army in the fifteenth century.

Those boys destined for the Janissaries were usually sent to work for two or three years without pay as agricultural labourers for Moslem provincial officials, while they learnt Turkish and the faith of Islam, and strengthened their bodies with hard physical labour. They were then returned to Istanbul, and divided according to strength and ability. Some went to serve in the fleet at Gallipoli, some joined the 1000 gardeners in the palace grounds, while others worked in shipyards or on public building projects. In due course almost all moved on to a period of military training before being enrolled in the Janissaries.

The Janissaries could be difficult to control, especially when unoccupied by war. They were notable for brawn not brains. They were physically trained far beyond their intellectual capacity, and idleness did not suit them. They lived harsh bachelor lives in uncomfortable barracks, on low pay. In wartime this was supplemented by their share of the booty, and in peacetime they could not always be restrained by their officers from looting cities where they were stationed. They elected their own officers from among themselves, apart from the *aga* (commander) who was appointed by the sultan, to whom he was responsible and from whom alone he took orders.

The Janissaries were the sultan's loyal fighting troops, but this did not prevent them from imposing their will on him. Their 'murmurings' helped Suleiman decide to raise the siege of Vienna, and to turn back from campaigns in Egypt and Persia. They could influence the succession by giving or withdrawing their support. No sultan reached the throne without the support of the Janissaries. After securing the accession of their candidate, the Janissaries demanded ever increasing donations as 'accession gifts', to guarantee their continued loyalty. Richard Knolles wrote in 1603 in his *'History of the Turks'*, 'Neither can any of the Turkic sultans account themselves fully invested in the imperial dignity or assured of their estate, until they be by the Janissaries approved and proclaimed.'

Even the great Suleiman, if de Busbecq is to be believed, trod warily in his dealing with the Janissaries. Busbecq's servants became involved in a quarrel with some of the soldiers and he complained to the Grand Vezir, Rustem Pasha, who replied by asking de Busbecq:

1 to remove every cause of offence which might occasion a quarrel
   with these atrocious scoundrels. Are you not aware that they are
   masters so that no one, not even Suleiman himself, has control
   over them, and is actually himself afraid of receiving violence at
5 their hands.?

By the time of Suleiman, there were nearly 14000 Janissaries. In peacetime about half were in Istanbul; the rest were stationed in the provinces, for part of their task was to enforce the sultan's orders outside the capital. They garrissoned captured castles, and, in the next century, towns and cities as well. They were also responsible for safeguarding the rights of Moslem subjects and ensuring that they were not victimised or oppressed by government officials. The Janissaries were not answerable to the local governor, only to the sultan, whose authority they represented wherever they went. This gave them great power, which, late in the seventeenth century, they were to abuse.

In wartime the Janissaries were the heart of the Ottoman fighting force, disciplined, professional fighters – a war machine without parallel in the west. De Busbecq, who had considerable opportunities to observe the Janissaries in camp and preparing for action, was greatly impressed by them. He compared them very favourably with the Christian armies.

1 On their side are the resources of a mighty empire, strength
   unimpaired, experienced and practised in fighting, a veteran
   soldiery, endurance of toil, unity, order, discipline, frugality and
   watchfulness. On our side is public poverty, private luxury,
5 impaired strength, broken spirit, lack of endurance and training;
   the soldiers are insubordinate, the officers avaricious; there is
   contempt of discipline; licence, recklessness, drunkenness and
   debauchery are rife; worst of all the enemy is accustomed to
10 victory and we to defeat. Persia alone interposes in our favour; for
   the enemy as he hastens to attack us must keep an eye on this
   menace in his rear. But Persia is only delaying our fate; it cannot
   save us.
15   The Turks take care to keep their soldiers in good health and
   protected from the weather – hence one sees them better clothed
   than armed . . . but they think only a coward finds fault with his
   arms, and prepare to fight. Such is the confidence inspired by
20 repeated victories and constant experience of warfare.

Elsewhere de Busbecq speaks of the ramshackle collection of body
armour and weapons with which the Janissaries were usually equipped.
Most of the soldiers had no armour at all, and for those who had, it was
usually ill-fitting, being in effect second hand, having been gathered up
on earlier battlefields or stripped from fallen enemies. Their main
weapon by the mid-sixteenth century was the cumbersome musket,
although they still used swords, bows and arrows, and spears from time
time. Attempts to introduce the more efficient smaller handguns were
strongly resisted by the Janissaries, as new-fangled and messy weapons,
and they did not come into full use until nearly the end of the
seventeenth century.
   De Busbecq was summoned to meet Suleiman during one of the
Balkan campaigns, and has left accounts of what he saw at the camp.

1 The first thing I noticed was that the soldiers of each unit were
   strictly confined to their own unit. Anyone who knows the
   conditions which obtain in our own camps will find difficulty in
   believing it, but the fact remains that everywhere there was
5 complete silence and tranquillity, and an entire absence of
   quarrelling and violence of any kind. You never see any drinking
   or gambling, which is such a serious vice among our soldiers . . .
   such is the powerful effect of their military discipline and severe
10 traditions. There is no crime left unpunished. The penalties are
   deprivation of office and rank, confiscation of property, flogging,
   and in extreme cases, death. On campaign the men take a small
   piece of canvas to use as a tent, some clothing and bedding, and a
15 private store of provisions consisting of a leather sack of the finest
   flour, a small jar of butter and some spices and salt. On these they

support life when they are reduced to extremes of hunger. They
take a few spoonfuls of the flour and place them in water, adding a
20 little butter, then flavour the mixture with spices and salt. This,
when put on the fire and boiled, swells up so as to fill a large bowl.
They eat it once or twice a day . . . and so continue to live on short
rations, for a month or longer.

Other European observers, who also wrote from a first hand
knowledge, agreed with de Busbecq in judging the Ottoman army to be
far superior to that of the Christians, as regards organisation, discipline,
bravery and fighting capability.

1 The Turks come together for war as if they had been invited to a
wedding; I think there is no prince in the world who has his
armies and camps in better order, both as regards the abundance
of victuals and other necessities, and as regards the beautiful
5 order and manner they use in encamping without any confusion;
The Turks surpass our soldiers for three reasons; they obey their
commanders promptly; never show the least concern for their
lives in battle; they can live a long time without bread or wine,
10 content with barley and water; Peace and silence reign in a
Turkish camp – such is the result produced by military discipline;
In truth, the discipline could not be better, or the obedience
greater.

⋆ As well as the Janissaries, the standing army of infantry, the palace
slaves provided cavalry troops, known as the Sipahis of the Porte
(horsemen of the palace). The Sipahis were recruited mainly from the
Janissaries, and officered by men selected from among the pages who
were not considered suitable for an administrative career. In the
mid-sixteenth century there were probably about 12000 of these
calvarymen. Their duty was to provide a bodyguard for the sultan in
peace and war. Busbecq describes them riding with Suleiman as he left
Istanbul at the start of a campaign. They were splendidly dressed in
robes of cloth of gold or silver, or else in silk or velvet, and with turbans
of white cotton wound round a 'fluted peak of purple silk' and
ornamented with black plumes. Each carried at his side a bow and
arrows in painted cases, a shield on the left arm and a spear painted
green (the colour favoured by the Prophet Mohammed) in the right
hand, as he sat, with his 'highbred steed, with trappings of gold and
silver, sparkling with gold, and with jewels in silver settings'. 'Round
his waist each wore a jewelled scimitar and at his saddlebow hung a steel
mace.'

In view of such united praise, it is clear that the Ottoman standing
army represented a powerful force, both inside the empire, where it
gave loyal and disciplined military backing to the sultan's authority,

and outside, where its reputation struck terror in the enemy before battle began.

3   The Timar System and the Feudal Sipahis

The *timar* system operated throughout most of the Balkans and Anatolia, but not in North Africa or Syria. Superficially, it appeared very similar to the feudal system of western Europe, but there were certain important basic differences. The *timar* system came into being as a result of the need to support a large army with the resources of a medieval economy. It eventually shaped the provincial administration of the empire, and dictated its financial, social and agricultural policies, all of which were designed to meet the military needs of the state.

At the end of the medieval period, the Near East suffered from a serious shortage of precious metals, which in turn led to a shortage of coin and the consequent problem of how to pay the army which was needed to embark on new conquests or to maintain control over newly conquered lands. Shortage of cash also meant that the peasants' tithes as well as other taxes had to be collected in kind. There was no means available to the state to convert these goods into cash, so the right to collect these sources of revenue was sold for a lump sum to tax farmers. This proved an uneconomic solution from the point of view of the state, which still did not have enough cash to pay the army.

A new scheme was therefore introduced by which the soldiers themselves were assigned the right to collect these revenues in kind, instead of receiving cash salaries. This was not a new idea. It was one which was already the established custom in other Islamic states, and was not unlike a system used in the Byzantine empire.

Under this new system the soldier, who would normally be a cavalryman, a *sipahi*, would be allocated land in a particular area where he would live, the revenues of which he would have the right to collect. He would collect the agreed taxes in kind. It was his responsibility to convert the taxes into cash, and to forward any surplus to the central government after deducting his expenses for the upkeep of himself, his family and his horse.

★The *timar* system gave the sipahi no rights of ownership over the land, which remained the property of the sultan. The *sipahi* was not a feudal tenant in the western sense, for the *timar* which he held was not the land itself, but the right to an income from that land, in return for which he agreed to present himself and his horse fully equipped for war, when called upon to do so by the sultan. Depending on the value of his *timar*, the *sipahi* might have to bring with him one or more additional horsemen fully armed and equipped. If a *sipahi* failed to fulfil his military obligations for seven years, he lost his military status and became merely one of the *reaya*, with a consequent loss not only of social status, but the loss of tax exemptions. A *timar* was only granted to an individual for life, and in the early period there was no hereditary element in the holding of the *timar*. However, it became normal in the seventeenth century for a son to expect to take over at least part of his father's *timar*. By then, though, conditions had changed, for the sipahis were becoming obsolete as a fighting force and the whole *timar* system was breaking down.

In the sixteenth century these feudal *sipahis* (so called to distinguish them from the Sipahis of the Porte) formed the largest part of the Ottoman army, totalling about 40 000 men. They were typical late-medieval cavalrymen, conventionally armed with sword, shield, lance, and bow and arrow.

★To establish the *timar* system it was obviously essential for the government to know the sources and extent of the revenues available to distribute as *timars*. Therefore, every 20 or 30 years commissioners would be ordered to hold local enquiries. They would make a list of available land, its occupier and its value. Subsequently, the level of tax for that particular district or village would be set. These cadastral registers were drawn up by central or local officials such as *beylerbeys* or cadis. They remained in force until the next survey was made. The peasants (the *reaya*) each paid a proportion of the total tax set for the area, and against which there was no appeal. In order to avoid disputes two copies of the register were made. One was kept centrally and one was kept by the provincial governor.

To make the system work the state had to own all the land involved. All rural land was declared crown land (*miri*), and under Islamic religious law all newly conquered land automatically became crown land. There was, in theory, no privately owned land, although some was illegally acquired by ambitious individuals and some was *vakif* (dedicated to pious use). Privately owned land could be seized by the Sultan's order. Mehmed the Conqueror went so far as to abolish all private ownership of land. He established the principle that any *vakifs* not sanctioned by the sultan should revert to state ownership. As a result over 20 000 villages and farms became *miri* land, and were available for distribution as *timars*. This in turn increased the number of *sipahis* who could be maintained and available for service in the army if required. By 1528, 87% of all land in the Ottoman Empire, where the *timar* system operated, was *miri* land. By the end of the century, as part of the general weakening of central authority, the state had begun to lose control of the *miri* lands, which fell increasingly into private hands.

Although the state owned the land under the *timar* system, the *sipahi* and the peasant both had simultaneous rights over it. It was not as is often incorrectly referred to by western historians that the *sipahi* was the 'landowner'. He was only the occupier for the time being. Acting as a sort of government representative, he was expected to enforce the state land laws, and to rent out vacant land in his area to peasants. In return the *sipahi* had the use of a plot of land for himself and his family. The size of this plot varied, in relation to the size of the *timar*, but was usually between 15 and 40 acres. When a peasant agreed to rent land he also agreed to cultivate the land continuously, to pay the fixed taxes, not to alter the use made of the land, and to accept that if he left the land uncultivated for three years it could be given to another. The peasant was a hereditary tenant of his piece of land, which was large enough to support a family.

In his capacity as a government representative, the *sipahi* was responsible for law and order in his area. He could arrest wrongdoers, but could not try them – that was the responsibility of the *cadi* (judge) – although he eventually received half the fine imposed. He could demand certain specified labour services from the peasants. These services were listed by the state and the *sipahi* could not legally introduce any extra ones, although sultans' decrees against abuses, especially in the seventeenth century, show that many did.

*To become a *timar* holder a man had already to be a member of the *askeri* (the military/ruling class). He could have inherited this status from his father, or could have acquired it as a slave of the sultan or of a senior government official. In the early days of the Empire, most *timars* were held by native born Moslems who had distinguished themselves in war, but by the late sixteenth century the great majority were in the possession of the sultan's slaves, many of them ex-Janissaries.

To obtain a *timar* was a lengthy business. A man who wanted one first obtained a recommendation from his commanding officer or from a local provincial official. Eventually an order would be issued in the sultan's name, stating that the applicant was suitable and giving an indication of the value of the *timar* to be granted. The applicant would then have to wait until a *timar* of the right size fell vacant. He would then, at last, receive a document of title issued by the sultan.

In order to gain new lands, there was a need for additional *sipahis*, who in turn needed *timars* to support them. It was a self-perpetuating case of supply and demand, at least until the end of the sixteenth century, by which time the Ottoman frontiers had reached a point beyond which they could not easily expand (see page 127). By that time other factors had changed the situation. Many *timars* were being distributed to non-military holders such as palace and provincial officials, or were being given in lieu of salaries. They were even being given to women and to members of the religious hierarchy. This was partly because the importance of the *sipahis*, not only as soldiers but also as government officials, was declining. As soldiers their usefulness was over. Their style of fighting was outmoded and was no match for new weapons coming into use among the enemy, while their law and order functions had been largely taken over by the Janissaries, who, without continuous war to occupy them, needed to be kept busy with policing and other duties in towns and cities all over the empire.

As the seventeenth century drew to a close, and central control weakened, the Janissaries stationed in the provinces disregarded the authority, not only of the local officials to whom they had never been answerable, but even that of the sultan himself (see page 70). The hierarchy of local officials, supervising the financial, judicial and agricultural needs of the provinces, collapsed. By 1700 real power in the more distant parts of the empire had passed into the hands of the Janissaries.

4 Social Structure

The Ottoman concept of the state embodied the principle that the defence and extension of Islam was paramount. As a result, the *sheriat* (the religious law) played a very important part in government from the beginning. Until the middle of the fifteenth century the vezirs and other senior officials were all drawn from the *ulema* (the religious hierarchy). Only after Mehmed the Conqueror greatly increased the use of the *devshirme* did the *Kul* (slave) system become the basis of government and the foundation of the bureaucratic system of the empire.

  * De Busbecq, that acute observer, wrote:

1 The Turks do not measure even their own people by any other rule than that of personal merit. The only exception is the house of Osman; in this case, and in this case only, does birth confer distinction; no distinction is attached to birth among the Turks;
5 the deference to be paid to a man is measured by the position he holds in the public service. There is no fighting for precedence; a man's place is marked out by the duties he discharges . . . It is by merit that men rise in the service, a system which ensures that
10 posts should only be assigned to the competent; they do not believe that high qualities are hereditary, but that they are partly the gift of God, and partly the result of good training, great industry and unwearied zeal . . . Among the Turks, therefore,
15 honours, high posts and judgeships are the rewards of great ability and good service. This is the reason they are successful in their undertakings, that they lord it over others and are daily extending the bounds of their empire.

Similarly, Menavino, a Genoese who was at one time a palace page, describes the slave system and proclaims its merits,

1 Out of the slaves, promotions are made to the offices of the kingdom according to the virtues found in them. Whence it comes about that all the magnates and princes of the whole kingdom are, as it were, officials made by the king and not lords
5 or possessors. As a consequence, he is the sole lord and possessor

and the lawful dispenser and governor of the kingdom. The others are only executors, officials and administrators according to his will and command . . . no contradiction, no opposition can
10 arise, but united as one man in all respects and purposes, they look to his command alone and obey and serve unwearyingly.

Menavino makes the point that senior officials were important only because of the posts which they held and only as long as they held them. It was their function in the state, not their ethnic origin, their language, their birth or their religion which placed them at the top of the social pyramid. They were made by the sultan and could be just as easily and quickly unmade if they ceased to be of use. Lower down the social scale the principle was the same; social status was determined by the relative importance and value to the state of a man's occupation. Once enrolled in any profession or craft or any other occupation, a man and his descendants, were fixed at that point on the social scale for all time (at least in theory, although later in the seventeenth century this rigid class structure broke down). At the very bottom of the social pyramid were those whose lifestyle contributed nothing to the welfare of the state – 'non-useful' persons such as gypsies and, to some extent, nomads, although these latter did have their uses as stockbreeders, providing horses and camels for the army and hides, wool and meat for the cities. An individual was of no value in his own right – only in relation to his contribution to the wellbeing of the state.

*As well as being divided horizontally by job value, the population was also divided vertically by religion. This had the effect of constructing a grid system for society, so that everyone lived within his own square, his *had*, the boundaries of which were determined primarily by his occupation and his religion. Everyone had his place – his own space – and for anybody else to trespass into it in any way was unforgivable. This had unfortunate repercussions in the provincial administration, where one official was powerless to intervene when it was clear that another was acting improperly, because to have done so would have been to invade the sanctity of another man's *had*.

The majority of those living within the empire were Moslems, either by birth or by conversion, but there were substantial minorities of Greek Orthodox Christians, Armenians and Jews and a number of other smaller groups. The different religions were organised into legally recognised communities called *millets*. Their members were free to live their lives according to their own religious customs and traditions, as long as they did not directly conflict with the wishes of the state. The Ottoman Empire was not only multi-racial, it was a generally tolerant multi-faith society (only the Roman Catholic church in the Balkans was proscribed, and that was for political reasons as it was the religion of the Balkan nobility). In some respects the Moslem peasant members of the *reaya* were better off than *zimmis* (non-Moslem subjects) for they paid lower taxes. Among the best off members of society, undoubtedly, were the sultan's slaves, for they formed the bulk of the ruling class.

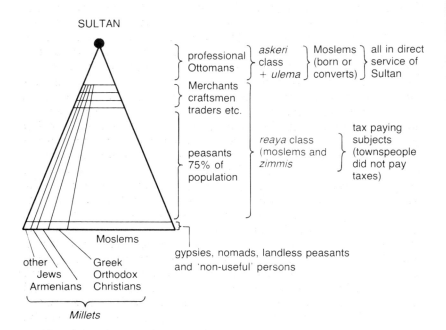

Intersection of social class and religious groupings in the sixteenth century

5 The Ruling Class

The Ottomans of the Ruling Class, both slave and free, were responsible for the government of the empire, both central and provincial, for its military organisation and for its religious and judicial wellbeing.

a) Government – The Central Administration

The Grand Vezir

The most important member of the administration was the Grand Vezir. The *Kanun-nahme* (Book of Laws) of Mehmed the Conqueror describes the Grand Vezir as 'greater than all men; he is in all matters the sultan's absolute deputy. In all meetings and in all ceremonies he takes his place before all others.' There were, however, some restrictions on his power. He could not, for instance, give a direct order to the *aga* (commander) of the Janissaries, who was answerable to the sultan alone, nor did he have complete control over the Treasury.

The Grand Vezir from the time of Mehmed the Conqueror was chosen from among the sultan's slaves. He would be a man of outstanding ability who had worked his way up the slave system, through various stages of promotion within the palace, and then outside it, in the provincial administration. One of the outstanding Grand Vezirs of the sixteenth century was Suleiman the Magnificent's close friend Ibrahim Pasha, who may have been his brother-in-law. He was born in Greece, the son of a fisherman. Captured by pirates and sold through the slave market of Istanbul to a widow in Anatolia, he was later presented as a slave companion to Suleiman, who was the same age. Handsome and intelligent, Ibrahim completed the page's training, and was promoted to chief falconer, one of the many functions within the palace Outer Service organisation, which was much more important than the name suggests. (The falconers were one of several departments in the Outer Service involved with military matters. Each of these departments had its chief (*aga*). These *agas*, known collectively as the *agas* of the stirrup, were entitled to ride beside the sultan on campaign, and could expect to be appointed as governors of provinces in due course.) He commanded a military campaign against Egypt, where he afterwards became governor, and he accompanied Suleiman to war on other occasions. He fought at the battle of Mohács in 1526, and, according to Suleiman's diary, later tried in vain to stop the fire which destroyed the city of Buda after its surrender. Ibrahim was cultured and intelligent. He spoke Turkish, Greek, Persian and Italian, as well as Ottoman. He was musical and played the viol; he read widely, especially history and he is usually said to have married Suleiman's sister, although recent Turkish research has cast doubt on this.

While he was Grand Vezir, Ibrahim was the most powerful man in the empire – and he knew it.

1 Although I am the Sultan's slave, whatever I want is done. On the spur of the moment I can give kingdoms and provinces to anyone I like, and my master will say nothing to stop me. Even if he has ordered something, and I do not want it to happen, it will not
5 happen; and if I command something should be done, and he happens to have commanded the contrary my wishes and not his are obeyed. I can make war and I can grant peace. I can make men rich.

Hearing this, a Venetian living in Istanbul remarked, 'If one day the Sultan should choose to send his scullion to slay Ibrahim Pasha, there would be no way of preventing the killing.'

There came a day when Suleiman *did* decide to kill Ibrahim, allegedly for attempting to gain control of the army and for signing himself 'sultan', but more probably because of pressure from Suleiman's scheming and devoted wife, Roxelana. In March 1536, Ibrahim was invited to dine with Suleiman and to stay the night at the palace as he often did. In the morning his body was found beside the outer gate. He had been strangled.

The position of Grand Vezir carried with it a high mortality rate. Selim I's vezirs carried their wills with them, just in case death struck suddenly – a wise precaution in their case, because he executed seven of them. Tenure of the post was short. Even if they were merely removed from office and not killed, few Grand Vezirs lasted more than a year. Those who did, like Ibrahim, or Suleiman's other important Grand Vezir, Rustem Pasha, enjoyed not only great power but also great wealth during their lifetime. Because he was a slave, all the Grand Vezir's possessions reverted at his death to his master, the sultan. It may have been that on occasions the benefits to be obtained from the death of a Grand Vezir swayed the sultan to order his execution. An inventory made at Rustem's death show his personal possessions to have included: 85 farms, 476 watermills, 1700 slaves, 2900 war horses, 1106 camels, 5000 embroidered coats, 8000 turbans, 3000 coats of mail, saddles and golden stirrups, 5000 books, 800 copies of the Koran and two and a half million ducats in cash.

*Rustem's incredible wealth is partly explained by his re-introduction of a tax on the great offices of state. This meant that the sultan took money for granting these offices. Soon, so did every official in the government hierarchy from the men immediately below him. A regular tariff was established, leading in time to a general acceptance of the need to give bribes as a means of advancement. 'Oriental monarchs are not to be approached without gifts', commented de Busbecq, but it was not only the sultan who expected such offerings. By the end of the sixteenth century, the Ottoman Empire has become notorious throughout Europe for the degree of venality among its servants, not only in the administration but in the judiciary as well. This was later to become a serious source of weakness, undermining as it did the established policy that appointments should be made according to merit and not according to the ability to pay. More and more rich and incompetent men attained high office as a result.

The Divan

The *Divan* was the Imperial Council, the chief organ of government. At the same time it was the high court of justice, being both a court of first instance and a court of appeal. It was not, though, a legislative body in its own right.

Until the late fifteenth century the sultan had presided in person over the twice weekly sessions of the *Divan*. A western observer described how Murad II had gone to 'a side gallery where his seat had been prepared. This was a kind of couch, upholstered in velvet and mounted by four or five steps. He sat on this, crosslegged, in the manner of his people'. The sultan would then hear complaints from petitioners. Cases covered by *sheriat* law would be referred to the *ulema*. Administrative matters would be referred to members of the *Divan*. Originally the sultan had heard cases sitting beside the inner gate of the Palace – the High Gate, or Sublime Porte. By the end of the fifteenth century the 'Porte' came to stand for the Ottoman government itself.

Towards the end of his reign Mehmed the Conqueror ceased presiding over the *Divan*, and the Grand Vezir conducted the meetings which now took place four times a week. The meetings were lengthy, seven or eight hours each, beginning at dawn and broken only by a simple meal of bread, meat, rice, fruit and water. At the end of the meeting the *Divan*'s decisions were written down and submitted to the sultan. Once he had approved them, the decisions were irrevocable.

The non-attendance of the sultan did not mean that he neglected his duties of hearing complaints. There was a small window, with a grating over it, high up in the wall of the Hall of the *Divan*, which opened into a room in the Mansion of Justice. Behind this window the sultan could sit unobserved and listen to proceedings in the hall below. (The Mansion of Justice was a tower building which formed part of the palace. It symbolised an early Ottoman idea that from a height the sultan could survey his domains and watch that no injustices were being committed against any of his people.)

1 The small square window serves as a listening post. It is a wickerwork grille, with a curtain of black crape or tafetta, and is called 'the dangerous window', because the sultan may, whenever he wishes, listen to and see all that takes place, without being seen
5 and without anyone knowing whether he is there or not. It would be extremely dangerous to conceal or hold back anything.

Murad III once left the listening post and took over the meeting, when he saw business being improperly conducted.

In the early days of the empire, the sultan would also hear complaints from people at other times, for anyone, of whatever social status, was free to approach him and to touch his robe on his way to the mosque on Fridays, or when he was going hunting. 'The people should feel that the sultan is concerned with their welfare.' By the middle of the sixteenth century this informality had given way to rigid protocol, and direct access to the sultan was very restricted (see page 61).

As the government's most important work was the administration of justice, this was the main function of the imperial council. But it also acted as a sort of cabinet, which discussed and then took decisions on all government affairs. It also agreed proposals for new appointments. The most serious discussions of all, the making of peace or war, were usually held in secret and separate meetings of the sultan with the grand vezir and other senior officials, including members of the *ulema*.

The Bureaucracy

A well organised and efficient bureaucracy supported the work of the *Divan*. It was needed to implement the decisions and to keep the records. There was a great deal of paper work involved and a large staff was required to deal with it.

In the sixteenth century the Ottoman civil service was in two principal sections: The Bureau of the *Divan* and the Bureau of Finances. The Bureau of the *Divan* was itself divided into three sub-sections. The most important of these dealt with the drafting, issue and eventual filing of all decrees, edicts and regulations (except for those dealing with finance), and all documents concerned with foreign affairs, such as treaties and capitulation agreements. The other two sections dealt with matters affecting government personnel, provincial and central government appointments, and with the distribution of *timars*. The whole Bureau was under the direction of the Chief Scribe. The Finance Bureau had many sub-sections and dealt with all matters of government income and expenditure. In time of war the staff of both Bureaux went with the army into the field to look after the paper work.

In Suleiman's time, the Bureaux were staffed almost entirely by Moslem-born men. Most were the sons or relatives of Bureau staff, and they were trained by the Chief Permanent Secretaries in a master–apprentice relationship. It was a lengthy apprenticeship in calligraphy, learning a series of different scripts, as well as the formats used for various sorts of documents. After a morning of professional tuition, the apprentices and secretaries spent the afternoon at the mosques in order to complete their Moslem education. Most bureaucrats would spend their entire career in the same Bureau, unless special ability or the help of an influential patron gained them advancement into the *ulema*.

Justice and the Learned Institution (the Ulema)

The *ulema* represented a different side of Ottoman government from that provided by the ruling class and was to some extent in competition with it. This was partly because it provided the best road open to ambitious Moslem-born men. It was a route that was not open to the sultan's slaves, at least in theory, although recent Turkish research has shown that there was not such a watertight division between the Ruling Institution and the Learned Institution as Lybyer propounded in his book on Ottoman government in 1913.

The importance of the *ulema* lay partly in Islamic religious belief that political authority was nothing more than a means of applying the *sheriat* to life. 'The state is subordinate to religion.' Membership of the *ulema*, like membership of the *askeri* (the military/ruling class), brought with it the practical financial advantage of exemption from paying tax.

The members of the *ulema* were the learned men who had passed through the Moslem educational institutions attached to the mosques, from the primary school, through college (the *medress*) to the law schools and universities. In the Ottoman mind, religion and justice were indivisible. Education was based on the study of Moslem theology and of the *sheriat*, while the law schools were supported by *vakif* endowments.

The *ulema* provided the scholars, teachers, lawyers and judges of the empire, each group organised within a rigid hierarchy of precedence. They were responsible for organising and propagating the Islamic faith, and for interpreting, applying and enforcing religious law in the courts and teaching it in the mosques and schools. They provided the judges (*cadis*) who tried the cases and applied the law, and the jurists (*muftis*) who interpreted it. The *muftis* would issue written opinions on questions which involved religious law.

The Chief *Mufti*, the *Mufti* of Istanbul, was the *Sheikh-ul-Islam*, the head of the *ulema*. He was outranked in any gathering only by the Grand Vezir and the Sultan.

1 The *Mufti* (of Istanbul) is the principal head of the Islamic religion, and is a person of great esteem and reverence, because he represents justice and the image of God. His election is solely the choice of the sultan, who chooses a man famous for learning in
5 law and eminent for his virtues and his strictness of life. The sultan will not oppose or contradict his decision. In matters of state the sultan demands his opinion. Scarce a vezir is proscribed or a pasha for crime displaced, or any manner of change designed
10 but the sultan arms himself with the *Mufti*'s decision.

Suleiman the Magnificent, hesitating whether to execute his son, Mustafa, or not, sought advice from the *Sheikh-ul-Islam* by putting to him a hypothetical case. Suleiman took the advice he was given.

b) The Provincial Administration

The largest unit of provincial administration in the parts of the empire which were under direct Ottoman rule, was the province. There were initially only two provinces, Anatolia and Rumelia, but they gradually increased in number, until by the early seventeenth century, there were 32. The provincial governor, the *beylerbey*, the 'bey of beys' worked through a council or *divan* like that of the sultan in Istanbul, with the assistance of financial and legal officers, secretaries and personal aides, who were appointed by the central government. His main duty was to collect court fines and all taxes not already assigned to *timar* holders. He was expected to send the surplus, after meeting his expenses including his salary, to Istanbul for use by the central government. It was assumed that there would be a surplus, and, until the late seventeenth century, there always was. The *beylerbey* was also expected to deal with matters arising from the appointment of *timar* holders, law suits involving members of the military class, and the enforcement and execution of all orders of the sultan.

The sultan's orders were passed down to the military governors (the *beys*) in charge of the *sanjaks* into which each Province was divided. The word *sanjak* meant a banner or standard. It was originally a golden ball on the point of a lance, which was carried before the *bey* as a symbol of his authority when travelling within his administrative area, which itself came to be called by the same name. The *bey* in turn transmitted orders to the *timar* holders.

The *bey* was assisted in his duties by a *cadi* appointed from Istanbul. The *bey* could not inflict any punishment without first obtaining the *cadi*'s judgement, but the *cadi* could not carry out his own sentences. The Ottomans considered this division of power essential to just administration in the provinces.

All officials, from the *beylerbey* down to the *timar* holders, were provided with an income (*dirlik*, literally 'means of livelihood') in return for their services to the state. In the sixteenth century experience in provincial administration was essential for promotion, and in the century before 1550 the road to become Grand Vezir was always through the provinces. Extensive research done by Metin Kunt shows how this was to change in the seventeenth century, as the importance of the *timar* system declined.

6 The Economy

a) Trade

Ottoman trade with Persia had flourished since the mid-fourteenth century. Luxury goods were imported through the port of Bursa, and commercial centres were built in western Anatolia. European merchants came there to buy cottons, silks and spices. Venetians in particular, came to Istanbul to trade. They settled there and in other cities of the empire, and in 1454 obtained valuable commercial concessions (capitulations). Other Europeans followed: Florentines, Genoese and French and later English and Dutch.

With the Ottoman conquest of Syria and Egypt, new short sea routes replaced the old overland ones to Istanbul for heavy goods, the trade in which was controlled by an Ottoman merchant company. It was the beginning of important developments in the internal trade of the empire.

The Ottoman conquest of the Balkans opened up profitable new land routes, as did the conquest of Persia and the lands in the east. There had been a threat to Ottoman involvement in the spice trade in the middle of the sixteenth century. The Portuguese, sailing from their bases in the Indian Ocean, had attempted to disrupt the old trade routes along which eastern spices reached Syria and Egypt, before passing through Ottoman hands into those of European dealers. Suleiman's efforts to dislodge the Portuguese from the Red Sea and Persian Gulf were only partially successful. Yet the spice trade, although much diminished, continued to be extremely profitable, and by 1564 it had even begun to revive to something approaching its earlier level.

But it was the work of Mehmed the Conqueror in creating the new capital of Istanbul that was all important. Trade was centralised on the capital because of the need to provide enormous quantities of food and other goods for the city, for the palace, for the army and for the bureaucracy. The palace records show receipts for wheat, tallow, cheese, fish, furs, salt, honey and butter (100 000 kilos of butter in a single order in 1600) from the Crimea, wine from Crete, woollen cloth from Europe, cottons and silks from the east, together with spices, rice, sugar and soap (50 000 kilos a year) from Egypt and Syria, and dried fruit and timber from Anatolia. There were two pricing systems, the going price in the market, and a price 25% lower, at which the government bought provisions for its own use.

Almost all the internal trade of the empire, and much of its external trade too, went through the capital, which was also the chief transit centre for luxury goods, and for cattle, sheep, horses and slaves. There was a brisk trade in slaves in the capital's markets, which brought in a substantial income for the government through a sales tax on each slave. All the empire's areas of production were focussed on Istanbul, and this did much to create a unified national economy of a kind unlike anything found elsewhere in Europe until much later.

This integrated economy was further developed by the state policy of regulation and control of all producers and retailers, in an attempt to prevent profiteering, and later, inflation. Food prices were fixed throughout the empire. The goods or produce were bought at source by state authorised merchants, weighed in state weigh-houses, and redistributed by the state to points of sale. Trade guilds exerted a powerful control over their members and over the production of goods, regulating the actions of the former and the quality and conditions of sale of the latter. Guild members in return received protection against outside competition. In the seventeenth century this tight control by the state and by the guilds proved counter-productive. It stifled new ideas and prevented the introduction of new methods of production. In true Ottoman fashion conservatism triumphed to the detriment of trade and industry.

The sultans used commercial privileges as a weapon in their dealings with European states. They granted and withdrew these privileges, particularly in furtherance of the French alliance and the pursuit of war with Venice. This policy sometimes rebounded on the empire, for the Ottoman economy was closely bound up in a successful trading relationship with western Europe. The Ottomans needed markets outside the empire for luxury goods, such as silk, cottons, wine, spices and furs. Later sultans encouraged an ever larger flow of European manufactured goods into the empire as a way of providing quick and easy additional customs revenue. This shortsighted policy eventually undermined the Ottoman economy. The Levant became an open market for western merchants, and more and more of the trade fell into foreign hands. Not only was this the case in the external trade with the west carried on by Venice, France and other countries which had been granted capitulations. Within the empire the Anatolian merchants from Bursa, who had dominated the internal trade in the fifteenth century, were being replaced by Armenians, Jews and Greeks a century later. The Ottomans were losing control of their trade and its profits. With the abundant influx of manufactured goods from Europe, the Ottomans saw no need to develop their own industries and there was no encouragement to try new methods of manufacture. The Ottomans fell behind very early in the march of industry.

b) Money

There had always been a shortage of precious metals in the area and sultans, from Mehmed the Conqueror onwards, found themselves forced to devalue the currency. They had to rely extensively on transactions in kind, rather than in cash (in the collection of taxes, for example), and to impose strict controls over the export of bullion. Egypt and Syria were the most wealthy areas of the empire and were vital to the Ottoman economy in the sixteenth century. Their budget surplus each year provided one third of the income needed for the whole empire. Even more important, the surplus was paid to Istanbul in gold, and not in goods. Without this source of bullion the Ottoman economy would have been in difficulties.

After 1580 the empire began to suffer from inflation. This was to have serious consequences in the next century, but in the fifteenth and sixteenth centuries there were no financial problems severe enough to prevent vast expenditure on that most expensive of all national pastimes, war.

Overview

The picture of the Ottoman empire in the fifteenth and sixteenth centuries is one of expansion and development, based on the driving and unifying force of Holy War. The near-absolute authority of the sultan, at the head of a strong and efficient central government (staffed by loyal slaves, a well organised provincial administrative and tax collecting system) was backed by a powerful disciplined army composed of both infantry and cavalry. In addition, the empire was economically stable and the sultan had become a power to be reckoned with on the European political scene. While the sultan was strong and able, there seemed no danger of the empire's collapse.

7 The Enemy

As well as the benefit of its own strength and unity in the fifteenth and sixteenth centuries, the Ottoman empire had the considerable advantage of facing enemies who were politically and religiously divided.

The Ottoman empire was militarily stronger than any single European state. The only chance which Christian Europe had to oppose the Ottomans successfully lay in combined action. This was something which did not happen. The crusading impulse had been severely weakened by the great Christian defeat at Nicopolis in 1396, and the pleas of the Bishop of Sienna in 1453, for international assistance from the Christian princes of Europe to save Constantinople, fell on deaf ears. Successive popes called for crusades against the Ottomans during the next century. They tried to rally the rest of Christian Europe to help Venice and Hungary in their struggle with the Ottomans and, in 1463, Pope Pius II even drew up plans with his two allies for the partition of the Ottoman empire. Nothing came of these papal appeals. The peace treaties of Madrid (1526) and Barcelona (1529) included clauses committing Francis I and Charles V to make a joint crusade against the Ottomans. But nothing came of these either. Although popes continued throughout the sixteenth century to press the idea of joint Christian action against the Ottomans, their efforts met with no success; the crusading age was over. It was a rare occasion on which the countries of western Euope agreed to sink their secular differences to fight together in the name of Christendom. When they did, as in the Holy League formed before the battle of Lepanto, the process was marred by jealousies and quarrels which threatened to destroy the enterprise before it began.

In the Balkans, the rift between the Roman Catholic bishops and their Greek Orthodox counterparts stood in the way of any united Christian action against the Ottoman armies there, particularly as the Orthodox bishops announced that, if it came to a choice, they would prefer the sultan to the pope. Roman Catholicism had been the religion of the Balkan nobility, and in many areas the Orthodox peasantry put their bishops' words into practice, and fought alongside the Ottomans against the Catholic armies of the Habsburgs.

The Reformation brought further divisions within Christendom, which were exploited by both the Ottomans and the Protestants. When Charles V was under pressure from the Ottoman armies in the Balkans, as in 1532, he would grant concessions to the Lutheran princes of Germany in return for short-term military help. When events were going well for Charles, as in 1546, he would take action to suppress Protestantism in Germany. At these times Suleiman sent messages of support to the Protestant princes of the Schmalkaldic League encouraging them to maintain their opposition to Charles and the Pope.

The growth of nationalism in the fifteenth century brought an end to political and military co-operation among the countries of Europe. The sixteenth century was dominated by the Valois–Habsburg rivalry. Both Francis I and Suleiman the Magnificent saw advantages in co-operation against Charles V. Francis declared:

> 1 I cannot deny that I keenly desire the Turk powerful and ready
> for war, not for himself, for he is an infidel, and we are Christians,
> but to undermine the Emperor's power, to force heavy expenses
> upon him and to reassure all other governments against so
> 5 powerful an enemy.

The French alliance became an important part of Ottoman policy, because it represented a means of harassing the Habsburgs, and at the same time ensuring that the Valois–Habsburg conflict continued. Francis was a willing partner in the Franco-Ottoman alliance. While a prisoner of Charles V after the battle of Pavia in 1525, Francis was suggesting to Suleiman that he should attack the Habsburgs in Hungary. As Thomas Cromwell remarked, 'No Christian scruple would deter the King of France from bringing the Turk and the devil into the heart of Christendom, if this could help him recover Milan.'

United action by western Europe against the Ottomans was clearly impossible during the first half of the sixteenth century. The Treaty of Cateau-Cambresis, bringing the Valois–Habsburg rivalry to a temporary end, might have enabled joint action against the Ottomans. But troubles at home, the Revolt of the Netherlands and the French Wars of Religion, prevented this, and no other countries were able or willing to take on the task. While alliances and leagues might be formed, they were temporary and fragile. They collapsed as soon as danger was past, as the Holy League did after Lepanto. The French advice to the sultan to divide his enemies and defeat each separately was superfluous; the enemies were already divided – Venice and Genoa, France and Spain, the Pope and the Emperor.

*The Christian armies of the sixteenth century are frequently described as weak and feeble. De Busbecq had no illusions about them, comparing them unfavourably with the armies of the Ottoman empire. Suleiman's armies did not lose a single battle, apart from the siege of Malta (1565), in over 40 years, a record which no European army of the time could match. His army was a homogeneous whole, well disciplined, efficient and brave; the Christian armies were composed of an *ad hoc* collection of mercenaries, mostly German, Italian, Swiss or Walloon, who would fight bravely for whoever paid them but who were not noted for their discipline. The Ottoman armies were well led. There was a clear chain of command, and no room for confusion. The

Christian armies had individually brilliant leaders, such as Don John of Austria, but little overall organisation. Disagreements and jealousies frequently delayed operations. The Ottoman armies were united by their loyalty to the sultan and by their faith in the teachings of the Koran that 'those who were slain in the cause of Allah are not dead. They are alive, and well provided for by Allah.' The Christian armies were not fighting out of loyalty to their king nor for their faith. The element of commitment was an important factor in Ottoman military success.

However, this was not enough, when, in the early seventeenth century, the Christian armies began to employ professional soldiers, new weapons and, above all, the new methods of making war – the art of strategy. The Ottomans, relying on traditional weapons, opposed to the use of firearms and following the old strategies that had served Suleiman so well, found themselves, in the late seventeenth century, no match for the Christians.

*The enemy on the eastern front was more difficult for the sultan to deal with. This was partly because the Persian Shah quickly appreciated the superiority of the Ottoman army in the sixteenth century and remodelled his own under a single command, and along similar lines. He also employed the one military strategy with which the Ottomans could not cope: mobility. He avoided long sieges and set-piece battles in which the Ottomans had the advantage of artillery and sheer weight of numbers, and followed instead a scorched earth policy over very difficult terrain. In addition, fighting the Persians meant fighting fellow Moslems, and this infringed *sheriat* law. In 1548 the Janissaries became unwilling to fight in Suleiman's Persian campaign, because they could neither plunder the civilian population nor enslave the soldiers they captured, since the enemy, even if heretical was Moslem.

There was one inbuilt advantage which the sultan's enemies possessed and which was never used effectively – that of forcing him to fight on two fronts at once. As a one-army state the Ottoman empire was geographically and politically vulnerable to a simultaneous attack on its eastern (Persian) and western (Balkan) frontiers. This was particularly so in the sixteenth century, when the sultan still led his troops in person. In 1533, 1548 and 1552, for instance, Suleiman was called away from campaigns in the Balkans by trouble with the Persians. On occasions like this the sultan would have to hurry with his army from one theatre of war to the other. He was always, however, able to arrange a treaty so that he could depart quickly from the other front, without leaving an unfinished war behind him. Although ambassadors and diplomatic correspondence were exchanged between the Shah of Persia and the governments of Austria, Venice and Spain on several occasions, negotiations to launch a co-ordinated attack came to nothing. No sultan had to contend with fighting on two fronts.

*One other advantage which the sultan's European enemies had over the Ottomans was the weather. Due to the distances involved and to the slow progress made by the army from Istanbul to the Balkan front, there was only a very short fighting season available each year to the Ottomans. This was only a few months at best; sometimes it was only a few weeks, before winter clamped down and the Janissaries had to return to the capital and the *sipahis* to their *timars*. The winter was too severe for the army to remain away from home – the horses would have died from cold and lack of food, many of the *sipahis* would have deserted rather than see their valuable animals die and the Janissaries would leave. It was the winter weather, not their army, which saved Vienna for the Habsburgs in 1529, by forcing Suleiman to withdraw. It was the same winter weather which set the westward limit to Ottoman expansion. Only a complete change in their military thinking would have enabled the Ottomans to move any further west, and it was not in the Ottoman character to make any such change. Although the weather in the Caucasus was equally severe, with deep snow, there were areas further south where the army could, and did winter. This meant an earlier start to the next campaigning season against the Persians, and enabled the Ottomans to move further east from Istanbul than would otherwise have been the case.

* While it would be wrong to ignore the weakness or disunity of their enemies in assessing the reasons for Ottoman success in the sixteenth century, it would be equally wrong to place too much emphasis on these factors. They did play a part in the empire's expansion, but not as much as some historians make out. The main reasons for Ottoman success in this period lay within the empire itself, in the quality of its leadership and its efficient military, political and economic organisation.

Making notes on *'Reasons for Ottoman Success: The Organisation of the State'*

The previous chapter looked only at the importance of the sultan in the success of the Ottoman empire between 1450 and 1566. This chapter is concerned with the other reasons for success – the organisation of the state. It deals with the military, economic and administrative strength which enabled the empire to overcome its enemies in both east and west during this time. As you read, try to arrange the reasons given in this and the previous chapter in order of importance. Which is the single most important reason, and why? The following headings and sub-headings should help you make notes on a rather complicated topic:
1.   Organisation of the state
1.1. The *Devshirme*
        The pages

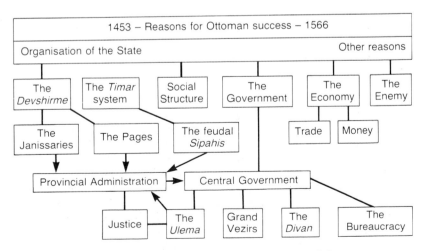

Summary – Reasons for Ottoman success: organisation of the state

Answering essay questions on 'Reasons for Ottoman Success: The Organisation of the State'

To answer questions on the expansion of the Ottoman empire between 1450 and 1566, you will need to use information from chapters 2, 3 and 4, because it is not possible adequately to discuss the territorial gains made by the Ottomans during that period without taking into account the reasons why they were able to make them.

You may sometimes be asked straightforward questions such as:

1. 'When was the Ottoman empire most dangerous to Europe in the period 1450–1566?' or
2. 'Why was the Ottoman empire able to expand so successfully between 1453 and 1566?'

Although the first question calls for factual knowledge of the events of the period, do not fall into the trap of writing a long chronological narrative. You are being asked to make a **judgement** about the time that was most dangerous for Europe, whether on land or sea. It is possible to write a satisfactory essay by choosing a single time, describing what was the situation, and explaining the ways in which it was dangerous to Europe. However, a more successful essay is more likely to result from a discussion of each of the main contenders for selection, with *pros* and *cons* explained in each case and a judgement made of the time which you consider to have been most dangerous. Draw up a plan for such an answer by listing the times of danger and noting both the nature and extent of each. Which was the most dangerous time? In what order would you present your points? Why?

The second question is a **'Why?'** question. As always, when dealing with a question of this type, make a plan based on a series of statements, all starting 'because'. In this case you might include:

1 because the sultans were strong and able leaders
   because of the well-disciplined Ottoman army
   because of the efficient organisation of the state
   because the Ottoman economy was sound
5 because the enemy was divided

In order to construct your essay you need at least three or four, and ideally, five reasons, each of which can be expanded into a full paragraph containing a range of detailed evidence to support your statement. Would you start with the most important or the least important reason? Why? The essay then needs a final paragraph in which you summarise your conclusions.

Many questions that initially seem complicated can be turned round and re-phrased in order to make the meaning clearer, for example:

3. '"The expansion of the Ottoman empire between 1453 and 1566 was the consequence more of its own strength than the weakness of its opponents." Discuss.'

This may seem daunting at first sight. But there is a simple technique for unlocking the meaning of a 'challenging statement' type of question. Turn it into a **direct question**, such as:

1 'Was it the Ottoman empire's own strength or the weakness of its enemies which was the most important reason for its expansion between 1453 and 1566?'

Once you have re-phrased the question you can see at once that you are actually being asked a sequence of questions. Here, for instance, you are being asked: What were the Ottoman empire's strengths? Were they the most important reason for its success? What were the enemies' weaknesses? Were they the most important reason for Ottoman success? Once you have identified the questions you are being asked it is a relatively straightforward matter to plan your answer. As you are planning your essay ensure that you also identify the **assumptions** that the questioner is making. In this case a number of assumptions are being made about the Ottomans and their enemies. What are they? They need at least a brief discussion. Last, but not least, in any question which includes dates, make sure your answer covers that time span adequately, but does not overstep it.

Reword the following questions to make their meaning clearer:

4. '"Europe had neither the means nor the will to resist the Ottoman advance". To what extent does this explain Ottoman success before 1566?'
5. '"The basis of Ottoman expansion before 1566 was the internal stability of their empire". Do you agree?'
6. '"Military excellence combined with religious devotion". Does this explain Ottoman expansion prior to 1566?'

What do all these questions have in common?

Questions on Suleiman the Magnificent occur fairly regularly at A-level. You may be asked to concentrate on his military successes abroad, on his achievements at home, on his 'magnificence' or, more probably, on all three.

Typical examples are:

7. 'Why was Suleiman "the Magnificent"?'

8. 'What justification is there for Suleiman's reputation as the greatest of the Ottoman sultans?'
9. 'How far does the reign of Suleiman the Magnificent illustrate the strengths and weaknesses of the Ottoman empire?'
10. '"Suleiman the Magnificent owed his splendour to much more than military achievements." Discuss.'

Question 8 makes an important assumption. What is it? It would be perfectly acceptable for you to make a discussion of this assumption the centrepiece of your essay. However, you would need considerable skill and confidence to do so successfully. A safer strategy would be to base your discussion on the four or five aspects of Suleiman's reign that mark him out as 'great', with a paragraph being devoted to each. What aspects would you choose? Would it be important to include in your essay aspects of Suleiman's reign that suggest he was not the greatest Ottoman sultan? Would you need directly to compare Suleiman with other sultans?

Question 10, is of the 'challenging statement' type, similar to questions 3, 4, 5, and 6. It could be re-written as, 'To what did Suleiman owe his splendour?' The original statement gives one answer – what are the others? The list you make will form the basis of your essay. The question requires you to do something more than list and describe the elements of Suleiman's splendour. What is this? In what order of importance would you place the elements you have identified?

Source-based questions on 'Reasons for Ottoman Success: The Organisation of the State'

1 The Janissaries
Read what de Busbecq and other western observers had to say about the Janissaries on pages 70–72. Answer the following questions:
a) According to de Busbecq, what were the chief reasons for Ottoman military success? How far are his conclusions supported by the other western observers?
b) Explain de Busbecq's comment that 'Persia is only delaying our fate' (page 71, line 13)? How accurate a judgement was it?
c) What ulterior motives might de Busbecq, as the Imperial ambassador, have had for contrasting the Christian armies so unfavourably with the Janissaries? Explain your answer.

2 Social Structure
Read de Busbecq's (page 76) and Menavino's (page 77) accounts of the social system, and look at the diagram on page 78. Answer the following questions:

a) What reason does de Busbecq give for the Ottoman success in extending their empire?
b) What, according to Menavino, were the consequences of the slave status of government officials?
c) What, in addition to their slave status, differentiated the Ottoman ruling class from that of western European countries?
d) Both authors write favourably of the Ottoman system. What arguments can be put forward against it?

CHAPTER 5

The Empire Continues 1566–1700

1 Suleiman's Successors 1566–1603

a) Selim II (1566–74), Murad III (1574–95), Mehmed III (1595–1603)

Suleiman was succeeded by his only surviving son, Selim II, known in both east and west as Selim the Sot (*sarhosh* Selim). (For details of Suleiman's other sons and the manner of their deaths, see Chapter 3.) At first, after Suleiman's death, the Ottomans hardly noticed any change. Military action was continued in Europe by land and sea, and even increased in the Mediterranean, conflict with the Habsburgs was maintained in North Africa, and campaigns were mounted against Russia and Persia in the east.

*In 1603 the Ottoman empire was still being called 'the present terror of the world' by Richard Knolles, the English historian, but as the seventeenth century progressed, foreigners and Ottomans alike began to say that, somehow the empire's Golden Age had gone, slipped away; no one could say exactly how, or when. Historians still do not agree on a date for the beginning of Ottoman decline. Traditionally western historians have given a date not long after the death of Suleiman. 1580 is the one usually chosen. Turkish historians see it as later, sometime in the seventeenth century, and this is a point of view which is gaining support in the west. Still unsettled is the precise date, because it must to some extent depend on what is meant by 'decline'. It is easier to point to a date when a decline has already begun than to say when it started, for a country's decline is not usually a steady, continuous downhill slide. It does not normally happen suddenly, through a dramatic disaster, but comes about gradually, through a series of events. This chapter looks at the external affairs of the empire, at its relations with its neighbours in the century and a half after the death of Suleiman, and tries to answer the question: when, in relation to foreign affairs, did the decline begin?

For a while, under Selim II, all went, apparently, well.

b) The East

Russia

The disruption of pilgrim traffic through Astrakhan brought repeated demands from the local Moslem population, as well as from the Moslem rulers of Samarkand and Bukhara in Turkestan, that as Protector of the

Sacred Cities, Champion of Islam, the Ottoman sultan should do something to help them.

The Divan, the Imperial Council, considered the matter. They turned down a proposal by the Tartars of the Crimea that there should be an immediate attack on Moscow, but agreed that there should be a strike against Astrakhan, combined with a project to construct a canal joining the Don and Volga rivers. This, if successful, would provide a safe waterway from the Black Sea to the Caspian, would keep the Russians out of the lower Volga, and would enable the Ottomans to threaten Persia from the north. The canal project soon proved a nightmare. 10000 fighting men, 3000 Tartars and 6000 labourers were transported from the Crimea along the Don, and in August 1569 began digging at a point on the Don nearest to the Volga. The work proved too difficult and the project had to be abandoned. It had only succeeded in uniting the Tsar and Shah in a proposed anti-Ottoman alliance and in the sending of an envoy from Moscow to Tabriz.

The commander who had accompanied the Ottoman army on its abortive canal-digging expedition decided that, rather than go home with nothing achieved, they should attack Astrakhan immediately, although it was almost winter. The attack failed, and the Ottomans withdrew dejectedly to Azov having lost many men and having to leave most of their cannon behind. Far from their base in Istanbul, the Ottomans were no match for the Russians in the cold inhospitable north and with inadequate lines of communication. For the time being the Ottoman government decided to leave resistance to the Russians in the hands of the Khan of the Crimea. When the Tsar stood for election as king of Poland, the Ottomans successfully backed their vassal, the *voivode* of Transylvania, against the Tsar, and then left him to fight their battles for them on the Tsar's western frontier.

Persia

Since the peace of Amasya in 1555 there had been no fighting of any significance along the Persian border. This tranquillity was broken in 1576 when a dynastic struggle threatened the internal collapse of the Persian state. The crisis was caused by competition for control between Turcomans, who had been the original supporters of Shah Ismail in the sixteenth century, and the more recently arrived Caucasians. The new Shah, a candidate of the Turcomans, tried but failed to stir up a religious riot in Ottoman Anatolia among his fellow Shi'ites. His subsequent actions in an area occupied by Sunni Moslems led the people there to appeal to Istanbul for help.

This seemed to the Sultan, Murad III, and his Grand Vezir a heaven sent opportunity to intervene, and the Ottomans embarked on a series of eastern campaigns which were to go on intermittently for half a century. Although under Islamic religious law, Moslem should not fight Moslem, the Sunni Ottomans justified their wars against Persia on the grounds not only that the Persians were Shi'ite heretics, but that Persia had become a militant state, which needed to be contained.

Campaigns in Persia had always been difficult. The journey was long and full of danger, the weather was bad, communications were poor and supply lines ill-organised, and the Shah preferred to follow a scorched earth policy which was difficult to counter by conventional means. The Janissaries disliked being so far from home, and had caused problems on all the previous Persian campaigns. For all these reasons it had always been impossible to win a rapid or decisive victory against the Shah. Ottoman military objectives and methods began to change in response to the problem. Their aim was to secure a permanent occupation of a limited area between the Black Sea and the Caspian Sea, by seizing and fortifying strategic strongholds. This would make the frontier secure, impose religious peace on the area, and give the Ottomans the rich silk-producing areas around the Caspian Sea, as well as extending Ottoman control over the important trade routes of the area.

From 1578–90 the Ottomans concentrated, therefore, on the Caucasus. They constructed a great fortress at Kars in 1579, and in the next five years built a string of defences on the routes leading to Tiflis. With the help of the Khan of the Crimea, they were able to keep control of an important port, Derbend, on the Caspian Sea. The campaign of 1585–8 had the aim of conquering Azerbaijan, and began by once again taking Tabriz. In 1586 the whole of Mesopotamia was annexed to the Ottoman empire. Four years later the new Shah, beset by internal feuds, made a peace treaty with Murad III. By its terms the Ottomans kept Tabriz, and all the western provinces of Persia which they had conquered.

c) Europe: The Balkans

The treaty between Selim II and the Austrian Habsburgs in 1568 had officially brought peace to Hungary, although border incursions and raids continued all along the frontier. By the early 1590s Ottoman raids from Bosnia into Croatia had increased greatly in number. In 1593 news reached Istanbul that a raid on Sissek in Croatia had gravely miscarried with heavy loss of life. Murad III was persuaded to seek revenge. A major offensive was planned, but this was no longer as easy to carry out as in the days of Suleiman. The Habsburgs had encouraged German, Hungarian and Slav refugees to settle in the frontier lands. In return for acting as guardians of the frontiers they were given religious and financial privileges. By the 1580s this had developed into a fully-organised military defensive system along the frontier, which the *ghazis* of Bosnia found provocative. A whole network of small fortresses protecting main routes and river crossings had been constructed on the Christian side of the frontier, in addition to the existing major fortified towns. As time passed, the Ottomans on their side of the frontier constructed a similar set of defences. The old fluid frontier was gone, and been replaced by a hard and fast line across which Moslem and Christian faced each other.

There were changes too in the fighting men. The Holy Roman Emperor had a substantial army of German, Walloon and Italian mercenaries, experts in modern warfare. The Ottoman historian Hasan-al-Kafi writing in his *Treatise on Government* in 1596 noted sadly that the Christians with their new types of handgun and cannon had now a great advantage over the Ottoman armies, where there had been difficulties in persuading the soldiers to use firearms at all. With the new style of fighting, the feudal *sipahis* were becoming outmoded and were being replaced by newly enrolled companies of Janissaries at the end of the sixteenth century.

The great Hungarian war, known as the Long War, which began after the debacle at Sissek in 1593, lasted for 13 years. It began badly for the Ottomans, as Moldavia, Wallachia and Transylvania, Ottoman vassal states, rose in revolt and went over to the enemy. This caused serious communication problems along the Danube, as well as the loss of supplies of horses, grain and meat from these provinces. A series of further upheavals and strained relations between Transylvania and Moldavia, as well as the armed intervention of Poland, ended happily with the return of Transylvania to the Ottoman fold. The war settled down to a series of long sieges costly to both sides in men and materials, so that the need for peace was felt by everyone involved. Both sides were exhausted, and the Ottomans were also worried about a new Persian initiative launched in 1603. The Treaty of Zsitvatorok brought peace to the Balkans in 1606 which was to last until 1642. The terms of the treaty, establishing as permanent the existing frontier, showed how the balance of power between the Ottomans and the Habsburgs had changed in favour of the latter. The days of the *ghazi* offensive were over. *Jihad* in the Balkans was no longer a practicable proposition. Ottoman expansion in the area was coming to an end; the frontiers were becoming fixed.

d) The Mediterranean

In the last quarter of the sixteenth century the English began to penetrate into the Mediterranean in search of trade. A London merchant, William Harborne, went to Istanbul in 1578 and obtained from Murad III a grant of capitulations (commercial privileges) similar to those which had long been enjoyed by Venice and, more recently, by France. Five years later he became the first English ambassador to the Ottoman empire.

Neither the Venetians nor the French were pleased to have a new rival trading in the empire. The Sultan, however, saw good reason to encourage trade with England, for that trade was in munitions of war and Ottoman losses of guns, smallarms and ammunition had been heavy in the long wars with Persia and in the Balkans. Cargoes sent out from England included large amounts of tin (needed for casting the great bronze cannon), iron, lead, sword blades, muskets, saltpetre and gunpowder. An Englishman, who had been a prisoner of the Ottomans from 1603 to 1605, wrote that the Janissaries 'had not one horn of good powder but that which they got from England' and that 'the English keep open three shops of arms and ammunition in Istanbul'. It was a thriving and profitable trade, and in addition Harborne and his successors were able to make good use of their opportunities to advance English anti-Spanish policies at the Sultan's court at the time of the Armada. Later they also encouraged the Sultan to embark on a Balkan campaign against the Austrian Habsburgs in 1593.

Cyprus

The conquest of Cyprus was the last great Ottoman military success. The island had been under Venetian rule since 1488, and it was never difficult to find excuses for a new war against Venice. There was always friction along the Dalmatian coast, and the use by Venice of Cyprus as a base for corsair attacks on Moslem pilgrim ships on their way to and from Mecca was a long standing grievance.

A formal demand from Istanbul that Venice should cede Cyprus to the Ottoman empire was, not surprisingly, rejected out of hand. Neither side was prepared for compromise, and the campaign against Venice began early in 1570, when Venetian merchants were arrested in Istanbul and in Greece, and two Venetian cargo vessels were requisitioned for the Ottoman fleet. Venice took fright and began to rearm. After nearly 30 years of peace, Venetian defences were weak, her system of fortresses outdated and her navy in disarray.

A powerful Ottoman force landed on Cyprus in July 1570. The support which Venice expected from her allies, Spain and the Papacy, failed to materialise. Divisions of interest in the Spanish and Papal fleets led to interminable delays, and before they could set sail came the news that Nicosia had been captured by the Ottomans. During the winter of 1570–71 a Holy League was formed by Venice and her two allies as an anti-Ottoman alliance, but by the time quarrels had been patched up and a combined fleet assembled at Messina, it was nearly the end of September 1571, and it was already too late to save Cyprus. Famagusta had surrendered and the Ottoman conquest of Cyprus was complete.

The Battle of Lepanto

Although it failed in its original purpose, that of rescuing Cyprus, the Christian fleet, under the command of Don John of Austria, the illegitimate son of Charles V, did achieve a brilliant naval victory, which practically destroyed the Ottoman navy on 7 October 1571.

The Ottoman fleet had been at sea since early in the summer, cruising round the eastern Mediterranean, making a few raids on the Dalmatian coast and on the island of Crete, and waiting to see what the allied ships were going to do. The two fleets were almost identical in size, around 200 ships each, almost all galleys, and evenly matched in fighting power. They came upon one another unexpectedly in the mouth of the Gulf of Lepanto in southern Greece. The Ottomans were outmanoeuvred early in the encounter and found themselves trapped in the long narrow gulf. From it only 30 galleys escaped. The remainder were captured or sunk, while the Christian fleet lost only ten ships. Casualties were heavy on both sides, for the rowers were very vulnerable to injury in any battle between galleys – more than half the total number of men involved in the battle were killed or seriously injured.

The Christian fleet could not follow up the victory by pursuit, partly because of its own loss of men, and partly because of bad weather. It was late in the year for further naval engagements, even in the sheltered Mediterranean, and Don John's suggestion of an immediate expedition to the Dardanelles received no support. By early November, all allied ships had returned home.

What had been achieved? The battle of Lepanto has been called by European historians 'the most spectacular event in the Mediterranean of the entire sixteenth century'. But the 'dazzling triumph of naval courage and technique' brought no practical advantage to the allies, and no lasting damage to the Ottomans. It was a glorious but empty victory, with nothing tangible gained and at great cost – as V. J. Parry wrote, 'a triumph symbolic in character, rather than positive in its actual consequences.'

It can be argued that its importance was its moral value. It gave Europeans hope.

1 The Turks are not insuperable as we had previously believed them to be . . . as the beginning of this war was for us a time of sunset leaving us in perpetual night, the courage of these men [Venetians who were killed in the battle] has bestowed on us the
5 most beautiful and joyous day.

So declaimed the Venetian historian who gave their funeral oration in St. Mark's in Venice. Lepanto was the greatest battle ever fought in the Mediterranean, and the last great clash of galley fleets in European history. It was the end of an age; naval battles were never to be the same again.

A year later, in 1572, the Holy League again assembled a large fleet under the command of Don John for another blow at the Ottoman power in the Mediterranean. The Ottomans meanwhile, by a super-human effort had, with the help of Algerian ship builders, created a new fleet of 200 ships equipped with modern weapons. After a few minor skirmishes in the central Mediterranean area, the two fleets met in earnest at the beginning of October off the port of Modon in southern Greece. Delaying tactics employed by the Ottoman admiral until the onset of the autumn gales forced the allied fleet to withdraw from the engagement and make for home, leaving the Ottoman fleet, if not exactly victorious, at least in sole possession of the eastern Mediterranean. For them Lepanto had been avenged.

*In 1573 Venice withdrew from the Holy League, exhausted, and made a peace treaty with the Sultan. By it she gave up Cyprus, agreed to pay a war indemnity and to reduce the size of her fleet. This peace was to last, somewhat precariously, for years.

e) North Africa

North Africa and the western Mediterranean in the earlier part of the sixteenth century had become as much of an Ottoman–Habsburg frontier as the Balkans, and this continued to be the case under Suleiman's successors. The Ottomans captured Tunis in 1570, but it was retaken in 1573 by Don John of Austria in a brilliant campaign. It was not, however, to remain long in Habsburg hands. The Ottoman fleet landed 40000 men unopposed in the summer of 1574, and, after a short siege, not only the town but the frontier fortress of La Goletta was taken.

This marked the end of the struggle between the Ottomans and the Habsburgs for control of North Africa. The Ottomans had won. Algiers, Tunis and Tripoli, the three great corsair states dependent on the sultan, became increasingly important as Spanish influence in the area declined.

The capture of Tunis, though, was another, less happy, landmark in Ottoman history. The victorious fleet returned to Istanbul in triumph – but it was the last triumphal entry an Ottoman fleet would ever make into the Golden Horn.

f) Assessment to 1606

The half century since Suleiman's death had been a time of mixed fortunes of war for the Ottomans. In the east they had gained Mesopotamia from Persia and in the Mediterranean had taken Cyprus from the Venetians, while in North Africa they had successfully thwarted the Habsburgs and extended their own sphere of influence. In the Balkans and in Russia things had gone less well. There, conflicts had ended, at best, in stalemate. In each case the Ottomans had failed to achieve their objectives and had suffered some loss of face, though not of territory. The battle of Lepanto had been a severe but short term defeat from which the Ottomans had made a remarkable recovery, leaving them a year later with no less naval strength than before.

On balance, while the days of *ghazi* adventure were over by 1606, at least in the Balkans, the Ottomans could be reasonably satisfied with the situation at the beginning of the seventeenth century. There were no serious signs of military decline.

2 The Seventeenth Century

Ahmed I (1603–17), Mustafa (1617–18), (1622–23), Osman II (1618–22), Murad IV (1623–40), Ibrahim I (1640–48), Mehmed IV (1648–87), Suleiman II (1687–91), Ahmed II (1691–95), Mustafa II (1695–1703)

a)The East: Persia

By 1603 Shah Abbas of Persia had overcome his domestic problems with the Turcomans and had built up a strong army of disciplined, well paid troops, recruited mainly from the Caucasus. He was ready to reconquer the lands surrendered to the Ottoman sultan in 1590.

The Shah began his campaign by an attempt, through English intermediaries, to form an anti-Ottoman alliance with several European states, including Venice, Austria and Spain. This attempt failed, mainly because of communication difficulties, but he was encouraged by Ottoman preoccupation in the Balkans and by news of a rebellion in Anatolia. He decided to advance his armies into the Ottoman-occupied Caucasus. There he had an advantage. The Ottoman occupation was not popular, nor well established and the loyalty of the majority of the population still lay with their former Persian rulers. Five years later Ottoman rule in the Caucasus was near to collapse. The great fortress of Kars and the city of Tabriz were back in Persian hands, and not until after peace had been made with the Habsburgs in the Balkans in 1606 could the Sultan, Ahmed I, turn his attention to confronting the Shah. The Ottoman army had little success, and the war dragged on.

The death of the Sultan in 1617, followed by serious defeat for the Ottoman forces, coupled with the lack of energetic leadership and a general loss of heart for continuing the war after years of ineffectual campaigning, led to the making of a peace treaty with the Shah. By its terms the Ottomans gave up all the land they had acquired in 1590 and withdrew to the frontiers which existed at the end of Suleiman's campaign in 1555.

These humiliating terms coming so soon after the acceptance in 1606 of a status quo in the Balkans are seen by some historians as marking the beginning of Ottoman military decline. The Ottomans themselves did not see it that way at the time. Their recuperative powers were always astonishing and, in the same way that they had rebuilt the fleet after Lepanto, they gathered and equipped a new army, and took the field against Shah Abbas. Again they were defeated. The Shah drove them out of Baghdad and Mesopotamia in 1623, but in that year a new Sultan, Murad IV came to the throne. He was energetic and able in the manner of the earlier warrior sultans, and under his leadership Baghdad was recovered. In 1639 a peace treaty with the Shah left Baghdad and Kars in Ottoman hands in return for the evacuation of Azerbaijan. Ottoman relations with Persia remained peaceful for the rest of the century.

b) The Mediterranean: Venice and the War of Crete

There was always a certain amount of friction along the Dalmatian coast between the Ottoman frontier *ghazis* and Venetian mercenaries, while in the Mediterranean, Venetian ships continued to fall prey to the corsairs of Algiers, Tunis and Tripoli. This accepted state of affairs was violently disturbed in 1638 when a Venetian ship was seized by corsair raiders in the Straits of Otranto. Another Venetian ship gave chase and cornered the corsairs in the harbour of the fortified Ottoman town of Valona. After a month's blockade, the Venetians bombarded the town, entered the harbour and made off with the corsair ships. Murad IV was still occupied with war in Persia and agreed to negotiate. He accepted compensation from the Venetians, and the matter ended peacefully.

Tension rose again in 1644 when the Knights Hospitaller, enemies of the Ottomans, captured a small fleet of Ottoman cargo ships, and sailed off with them to the Venetian island of Crete, where they were given sanctuary. This aroused anti-Venetian feelings in Istanbul, and the winter of 1644–45 was filled with preparations for war. In June 1645

Ottoman troops landed in Crete. This was the beginning of a very long war with Venice, which was to last for over 20 years.

At first the war went in favour of the Ottomans, partly because the repressive rule of Catholic Venice over the Greek-speaking Greek Orthodox population of Crete meant that there was no popular support for the Venetian forces defending the island, which were centred on the defence of Candia, the one great fortified base there.

In 1656 the Venetians destroyed the Ottoman fleet in a battle off the Dardanelles, and afterwards seized the important islands of Lemnos and Tenedos nearby. The Ottoman defeat was not entirely unexpected as the newly appointed grand admiral had no naval experience and owed his appointment solely to the fact that he was the Sultan's brother-in-law.

Panic broke out in Istanbul when it was realised that the Venetians had taken the two islands, for the Dardanelles could now be blockaded, cutting off supplies to the capital. Prices rose, people fled the city and various officials, including the religious leader, the *Sheikh-ul-Islam*, were made scapegoats and executed. The Sultan, Mehmed IV, spent his days hunting, and only the appointment of Mehmed Köprülü as Grand Vezir saved the empire (for the Köprülü family see Chapter 6, page 134).

Under the personal supervision of Köprülü, the Ottoman fleet was again rebuilt, and within a year the two islands had been recovered. The danger to Istanbul had been removed, the state of emergency was over, but the war in Crete dragged on. Candia had been heavily fortified by the Venetians at the beginning of the war, and all attempts to take it had failed. The next Grand Vezir, Ahmed Köprülü, began a siege of the fortress in 1667 in an all out attempt to win the war. Two years later, the Venetians surrendered Candia.

Once the conquest of Crete was complete, the eastern Mediterranean effectively became an Ottoman lake. Ottoman influence had been extended and strengthened in the area, for they had gained an important military base and a useful centre of trade. Venice's influence had been correspondingly weakened.

c) The Balkans: Ottoman–Christian Relations

Between 1617 and 1655, all was quiet in the Balkans. A short war against Poland, which brought no profit to the Ottomans, was the only conflict with a Christian state during these years. The involvement of Austria in the Thirty Years War (1618–48) and the long Ottoman war against Persia (1623–39) followed by the even longer war against Venice in Crete (1645–67) meant that neither side sought a major action along the Danube. Although minor outbreaks of guerilla-type fighting continued intermittently, it was not until 1656 that any serious conflict took place.

Despite this period of official peace along the Ottoman–Christian Danube frontier, the old idea of a European crusade against the Ottomans was still a lingering dream, which gained impetus from the Catholic revival of the Counter Reformation. A large number of quite impracticable schemes were proposed by central Europeans, some of them based on support for 'pretenders' to the sultan's throne, others centred on exploiting possible local resistance to Ottoman rule in some of the more isolated Christian areas of Albania and Montenegro. A scheme for invading Albania was drawn up in 1640, which involved the capture of several fortresses, a mass Christian uprising, the occupation of strategic routes, and a 'breakout' to the east, leading to a lightning advance on Istanbul!

The chances of this or any other such expedition materialising was very small. The states of western Europe were too much concerned with their own affairs to be interested, and in any case most of them were involved in the Thirty Years War. Even if such a 'crusade' had been mounted, it is very doubtful if any support would have been available from Christian resistance groups in Albania. The Christians there were much more concerned with defending their own local customs and traditions than in joining in any general crusade.

On the whole, Moslem and Christian were prepared to live and let live, even if the reasons for doing so were due to military and economic factors, rather than to religious toleration.

Hungary
In the early 1660s the Ottomans once again came into conflict with Hungary. In 1661 the Grand Vezir Ahmed Köprülü led an Ottoman army to Belgrade to assert Ottoman authority. From there he issued a series of demands to the Austrians. When these were refused, he put himself at the head of 10 000 men (gone were the days of the sultan riding at the head of his troops) and marched through Buda, into northwest Hungary, which was the part of the country still under Austrian rule. There was little resistance and Ahmed returned victorious to Istanbul.

This new surge of Ottoman military power greatly alarmed western Europe. Catholic France and Spain sent reinforcements to assist the Austrians, and, under the leadership of the Pope, a Holy League was formed against the infidel. Despite these reinforcements, when Ahmed returned to the Danube in 1664 with a large army, the Austrians were not prepared to fight, and a peace treaty was negotiated. By it the Ottomans gained two fortresses, while the Austrians kept western Hungary.

Transylvania and Poland
During the early seventeenth century Ottoman control over their vassal state of Transylvania had become weak, and the Prince of Transylvania

made several attempts during the 1650s to free his country completely from Ottoman rule. This was a serious worry to the Ottomans, for Transylvania was a bridge between Hungary and Poland, and therefore important in any possible future plans for Ottoman expansion. It was important too as a buffer state protecting the Ottoman empire from attack from the north. After the Prince of Transylvania attempted to make himself King of Poland in 1655, the Grand Vezir Ahmed Köprülü led the Ottoman army against the unruly vassal prince, who was defeated in the resulting battle, and died of wounds shortly afterwards.

Peace was restored to Transylvania, while the Ottoman army went on to take two fortresses on the Dneiper River, and to advance deep into Poland. By the peace treaty of 1676, the Ottomans kept the two fortresses and the whole of Podolia (southern Poland). This was to be the furthest territory north and west of the Black Sea ever conquered and settled by the Ottomans.

d) Assessment to 1680

These successes in Hungary, Crete and Poland give the lie to the long held western view that the Ottoman empire was in general military decline by the beginning of the seventeenth century, if not earlier. It is not until the last quarter of the seventeenth century that Ottoman successes begin to be outnumbered by failures. The 1660s and 1670s are a watershed. They mark the division between the expanding and the declining empire, and between victory and defeat. They were a time when Ottoman prestige was riding high and Turcophobia broke out again in central Europe as it had in the previous century. European observers spoke of the empire being invested with a new power and glory by the Köprülü family, such as had not been seen since the days of Suleiman the Magnificent.

3 The Beginning of Decline 1680–1700

The Second Siege of Vienna

In 1682 the latest member of the Köprülü family to become Grand Vezir was the warlike Kara Mustafa. In his search for glory, he set his sights on achieving an outstanding conquest – that of Vienna, called by the Ottomans 'the Red Apple', which Suleiman had failed to take in 1529. Success there would set the seal on the Köprülü family's restoration of Ottoman power, and mark it as permanent. Failure could mean ruin for Kara Mustafa himself and for his family.

The treaty with Austria in 1664 was due for renewal. Köprülü took an intransigent stand in the negotiations, which as he had intended broke down. In the name of the sultan he declared war:

1 You have for some time past acted to our prejudice and violated

our friendship, although we have not offended you, neither by
war, nor otherwise; but you have taken private advice with other
kings and your councils how to take off your yoke, in which you
5 have acted very indiscreetly, and thereby have exposed your
People to fear and danger, having nothing to expect but death
which you have brought upon yourselves. For I declare unto you
that I will make myself your master, pursue you from east to west
10 and extend my Majesty to the end of the earth; in all of which you
shall find my power to your great prejudice. I assure you that you
shall feel the weight of my Power; and for that you have put your
hope and expectation in the strength of some towns and castles, I
15 have given the command to overthrow them, and to trample
under foot with my horses all that is acceptable and pleasant in
your eyes, leaving nothing hereafter by which you shall make a
friendship with me, or any fortified places to put your trust in;
20 For I have resolved without retarding of time to ruin both you
and your people, to take the German Empire according to my
pleasure, and to leave in the Empire a Commemoration of my
dreadful Sword, that it may appear to all; it will be a pleasure to
25 me to give a public establishment of my religion, and to pursue
your Crucified God, whose wrath I fear not, nor his coming to
your assistance, to deliver you out of my hands. I will according
to my pleasure put your Sacred Priests to the plough and expose
30 the Breasts of your Matrons to be sucked by dogs and other
beasts.
　　You will do well to forsake your Religion, or else I will give the
Order to Consume you with Fire. This is enough said unto you,
35 and to give you to understand what I would have, in case you have
a mind to know it.

Köprülü gathered his forces. Contemporary Ottoman historians give
the numbers of troops at 500 000, but it was certainly far fewer than
that. A realistic figure, given by the chroniclers, is around 200 000. This
accords with the known resources of the empire. Many of these men
were not in fact soldiers, but were artisans, tradesmen and servants. All
these, plus enormous numbers of pack animals, combined to make the
army look much larger than its fighting strength of probably 90 000.
　　Without waiting to take two fortresses which barred the direct route
to Vienna, Köprülü marched north and arrived in July 1683 outside the
gates of the city. In true Moslem tradition, he had a message fired into
the city by an arrow, inviting the inhabitants to surrender and accept
Islam, or to perish by the sword. No answer being received, the
Ottomans settled down to a siege. The city with its strong fortifications
was, by seventeenth century standards, easy to defend and difficult to
conquer. But the Ottomans had arrived more quickly than expected
and before the inhabitants were ready for an attack. Preparations were

not complete and there were only about 12 000 soldiers inside the walls. The Austrian Emperor and his family had fled with their court as the Ottomans advanced, and most of the Austrian army had quietly retired to places of safety higher up the Danube.

The Ottoman army began an attack with cannon, but their lack of heavy guns made it impossible to breach the defences, and continued sorties by the defenders harassed the sappers, preventing them from undermining the walls successfully. As the siege dragged on, many of the Ottoman soldiers, who had collected enough booty on the outward journey, became restive and anxious to return home. A concentrated all out attack might have taken the city, but Köprülü left it too late. Assistance from various parts of Europe had arrived – from the Pope, from Italian and German states and from the King of Poland who came with 20 000 men. The latter promptly took command of the defending army across the river, and which now included the Austrians themselves. Louis XIV did nothing to help. It was in his interests to see the Habsburgs defeated by the Ottomans, just as it had been in the interests of Francis I.

On 12 September 1683 the combined Christian army crossed the River Danube and drove the Ottoman army out of their encampment, where they captured a great deal of booty. Against the allies' heavy artillery, who was now brought into use, Köprülü could do nothing but order a retreat. This quickly became a rout all the way back to Belgrade. There he regrouped what remained of his army. He planned to winter there and to launch another attack in the spring. When the news reached the Sultan's palace in Istanbul there was deep gloom. Mehmed even gave up hunting, his one real interest in life. A scapegoat for this unparalleled disaster had to be found, and the whole blame for the defeat was laid on Köprülü. The Sultan disclaimed all knowledge of any proposed attack on Vienna, and denied that Köprülü had consulted him (there is no evidence whether this was so or not). He argued that Köprülü had, therefore, acted treasonably by attacking Vienna without proper authority, and ordered his execution. Köprülü was strangled in Belgrade on Christmas Day 1683.

His death was a great loss to the empire, for despite his failure to take Vienna, he was the only man capable of leading the army, and, as many senior officials admitted, the only man capable of taking revenge on the enemy.

The Aftermath of Vienna

The immediate result of this Ottoman catastrophe outside Vienna was the occupation of part of Ottoman Hungary by the Austrians. Within a month they had advanced along the upper Danube, occupying fortresses as they went. In the spring of 1684 another Holy League was formed to take advantage of Ottoman discomfiture. With the support of the Pope, its members Austria, Poland and Venice began to dismember the

Ottoman Balkan territories. The Venetians occupied the Dalmatian coast and the Morea in southern Greece, from which they threatened Ottoman shipping, as they had done in the sixteenth century. They also retook Athens. It was during this bombardment that the Parthenon was largely destroyed. The Austrians drove further into Hungary, retaking Buda in 1686 after a short siege, while Poland struck south towards the Black Sea coast. In 1687 Russia joined the allies and launched an attack on the Crimea. In December of that year the coronation of the Archduke of Austria at Buda as King of Hungary was a severe blow to Ottoman pride.

To make matters worse for the Ottomans it was a time of drought and famine in Anatolia. Public discontent and disorder grew, while Mehmed continued unconcerned. He had resumed his daily occupation of hunting. In Istanbul the citizens were saying that the empire was lost, but that the Sultan did not care. The Grand Mufti warned Mehmed that unless he gave up his insatiable passion for hunting, and devoted his attention to affairs of state, there would be a rebellion. For a whole month the Sultan managed not to go hunting, but then announced that he could not continue to live without indulging his obsession. Hearing this, the army joined with the *ulema* in denouncing the Sultan as unfit to rule. Mehmed took fright, promised never to hunt again, sold his horses, gave away his hounds and closed down his stables. He agreed to cut down on palace expenses and, as a gesture of good faith, dismissed several hundred women of the harem. However, it was too little, too late. In November 1687 the army mutinied, marched on Istanbul and deposed the Sultan. He remained a prisoner in the cage for the last five years of his life. His brothers, Suleiman II (1687–91) and Ahmed II (1691–95) succeeded him, followed by his son, Mustafa II (1695–1703).

The empire appeared to be disintegrating. Internal unrest and external defeat combined to create what appeared to be insuperable difficulties. Such relief as there was came from two sources: events in Europe and the arrival on the scene of yet more members of the Köprülü family.

In the last years of the seventeenth century a number of events distracted European attention from the weakness of the empire. The Revolution of 1688 in England and the outbreak of the Nine Years War in the same year involved most of western Europe, while the death of Pope Innocent XI in the following year deprived the Holy League of its driving force.

The next Köprülü, Fazil Mustafa, was appointed Grand Vezir and commander of the army in 1689. He restored some degree of order at home and began preparations for a campaign in the Balkans. It seemed a propitious moment for an Ottoman attack. The Hungarians had become restless under Austrian rule, and much of the Austrian army had been redeployed to meet the threat from Louis XIV in the west. In

1691 Köprülü led the army to the recapture of Belgrade, but before he could advance into Hungary he was killed in battle and his army was severely mauled. Peter the Great of Russia took advantage of the confusion which followed this defeat to attack the Crimea, and in 1696 took the port of Azov in a surprise attack. It was the first military victory by the Russian army over the Ottomans. In the east, which had been quiet for many years, there was trouble from nomadic Arabs and Turcoman tribesmen, who captured the city of Bursa. Although it was soon returned to the Ottomans, the nomads continued to disrupt caravan routes between Aleppo and Baghdad, so that much of the trade was diverted to Persia and away from Istanbul.

With the accession of Mustafa II in 1695 there was to be a brief resurgence of military glory. A few small places in the Balkans were recovered from the Austrians amidst great applause at home. It was not to last. In 1697, Mustafa, encouraged by his officials to see himself as a *ghazi* warrior, insisted on leading his army in person to recover Hungary, something he was ill-equipped to do. Plans were badly made and there was discord among the army commanders. Marching northwards through the swampy country of the Banat in southern Hungary, the Ottomans planned a surprise attack, but were themselves surprised by Austrian troops. Caught with their cavalry and infantry on opposite sides of the river Tisza, the Ottomans were heavily defeated in what the Austrians themselves called 'this frightful blood-bath'. The Ottomans lost about 35 000 men. The Janissaries immediately mutinied and executed the Grand Vezir. By the end of the summer the Austrians had advanced unopposed far into Bosnia and were plundering the town of Sarajevo.

The Treaty of Karlowitz, 1699
The Grand Vezir appointed to replace the one executed by the Janissaries, was yet another Köprülü, Hussein Pasha. He had enough common sense to realise that, with the army in ruins and the empire in need of a respite from war, he must make peace. With the help of the English and Dutch ambassadors in Istanbul, he made contact with the enemy at Karlowitz, a small town in Croatia. There the Sultan's envoys bargained with Austria, Poland, Russia and Venice. Eventually, after long and difficult negotiations, a peace treaty was drawn up on the basis of *uti possedetis* (a Latin phrase meaning that each side would keep what it possessed at the time of the treaty).

The treaty was signed on 27 January 1699. It is significant as the first agreement between the Ottomans and a European coalition, and as the first occasion on which the Ottomans made use of neutral ambassadors as mediators. But most of all, it was the first occasion on which the Ottomans formally acknowledged a defeat.

By the terms of the treaty the Ottomans lost Hungary and most of Transylvania to Austria; Dalmatia and the Morea to Venice, and

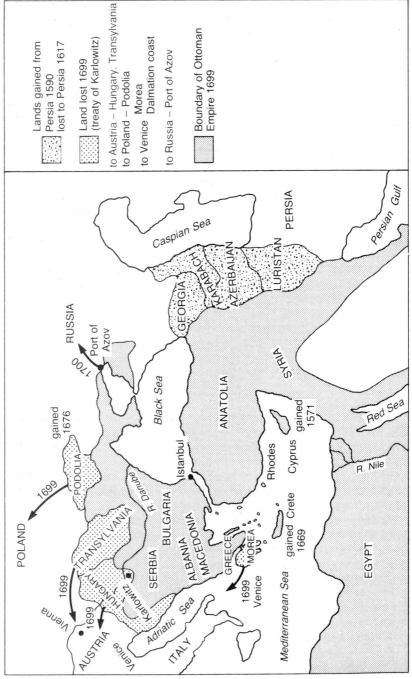

The Ottoman Empire in 1700

Podolia to Poland. By a further treaty a year later, the Ottomans ceded Azov to Russia and agreed to a Russian ambassador being appointed to Istanbul. The Sea of Azov was no longer an Ottoman lake.

a) Assessment: 1700

There can be no doubt that by 1700, if measured in terms of military success and international prestige, the decline of the Ottoman empire had already begun. The defeats of the last two decades of the seventeenth century far outweighed any successes, and the humiliating terms of the Treaty of Karlowitz would have been unthinkable, even 30 years earlier. There were to be periods of partial and temporary military recovery during the eighteenth century, but the heady days of expansion and perpetual victory were gone for ever. The empire was beginning to shrink, at least in the west; the Ottomans were retreating from Europe – the 'Great Fear' was over.

If we place the beginning of decline between 1680 and 1700, we can say *when* it happened. But we also need to ask *why* it happened. This is a much more complex question, and the answer depends on developments within the empire during the seventeenth century. These are dealt with in Chapter 5.

Making notes on 'The Empire Continues'

This chapter is in two parts, dealing first with Suleiman's successors in the second half of the sixteenth century and then with the seventeenth century. The important question raised concerns the date of the Ottoman decline, and in making your notes you need to be sure that you understand the arguments for and against the traditional date of 1580 as opposed to one about a century later. Again, making a simple time chart under the heading the Balkans; the Mediterranean and North Africa; the East, as you did for Chapter 2, would be sensible. The following headings and sub-headings should help you in making your notes:
1. Suleiman's successors
1.1. The date of decline?
1.2. The East
      Russia
      Persia
1.3. Europe: The Balkans
1.4. The Mediterranean
      Cyprus
      Lepanto

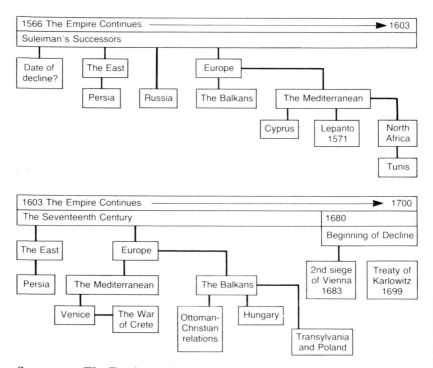

Summary – The Empire continues

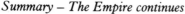

Answering essay questions on 'The Empire Continues'

Questions on Suleiman's successors (i.e. the second half of the sixteenth century) tend to concentrate on naval activities in the Mediterranean, particularly on the battle of Lepanto (1571).
These are often straightforward:

1. 'Was Lepanto an "empty victory"?' or
2. 'Was the battle of Lepanto a turning point in European history?'

Questions of this type can be answered in three different ways – 'Yes, because . . .', 'No, because . . .', or more often, 'On the one hand, yes, because . . . but, on the other hand, no, because . . .' The main danger to avoid is picking on the key word 'Lepanto' and launching into a narrative account. The examiner is hoping for an **analytical** approach, giving a reasoned argument as to the decisiveness or otherwise of the battle.
Questions on the seventeenth century Ottoman 'threat to Europe' are usually based on the activities of the Köprülü family (1659–1700). For example:

3. 'How far did the Ottomans continue to threaten Europe during the Köprülü era?'
4. 'To what extent were the Ottomans a serious threat to the Habsburgs between 1648 and 1699?'

'How far' and 'To what extent', questions are essentially the same. They normally require a two-part answer. The first part of the essay sets out reasons for saying, 'This far, or to this extent, yes', while the second part looks at reasons for saying, 'This far, or to this extent, no.' The essay should finish with a paragraph setting out the conclusions (i.e. the relative strength of the 'yes' and 'no' arguments) to be drawn from the information you have presented.

Source-based questions on 'The Empire Continues'

1 Vienna, 1683
Read the contemporary English translation of the declaration of war sent by Köprülü to the Emperor (page 107–8). Answer the following questions:
a) What was the 'yoke' which the Austrians had been trying to take off (line 4)?

b) What is meant by 'the weight of my Power' (line 12)?
c) What threats are made against the Christian church? In what ways were these in contrast to normal Ottoman policy in such matters? Explain this discrepancy.
d) What possible purposes could declarations of war of this type serve? Explain your answer.

CHAPTER 6

Reasons for the Decline of the Ottoman Empire

1 The Date of the Decline

Western historians still tend to choose a date for the beginning of the decline of the Ottoman empire soon after the death of Suleiman the Magnificent, or even a little earlier, on the grounds that signs of decline were already visible before 1566. Yet to most Europeans and to almost all Ottomans it was not apparent at the time that there was any decline at all in the empire's power or prestige until more than 100 years later, in the last quarter of the seventeenth century. As far as Ottoman relations with the outside world are concerned, the date may reasonably by set between 1680 and 1700.

The traditional western view is that the decline of the Ottoman empire was rapid, continuous and inevitable. This view is an oversimplification. That there *was* an eventual decline is not in dispute, and the causes of that decline are to be found in developments within the empire itself. Whether it was rapid, continuous or inevitable is, however, open to question.

a) The Ottoman View

The political theory of the state common to the near and middle eastern countries from early times was the so-called Circle of Equity. This was a

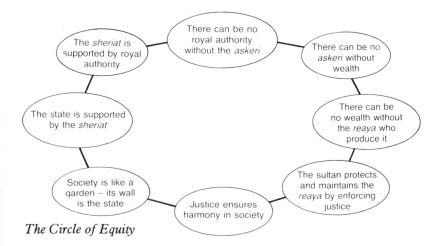

The Circle of Equity

series of phrases, written around the circumference of a circle, and intended to show a circular relationship and interdependence between the various social classes and their functions within the state. It is usually given in the general form shown on page 117.

The whole ethos of the Circle of Equity was based on the essential difference between the *askeri* (the military/ruling class) and the *reaya* (tax paying subject class).

In his influential *Book of Counsel for Vezirs and Governors* Sari Mehmed Pasha wrote:

> 1 It is necessary to avoid carefully the introduction of the *reaya* into the *askeri* class . . . for if the entrance of the *reaya* into the *askeri* class becomes necessary, the *reaya* are diminished in number, and the way is paved for a reduction in treasury receipts. Through
> 5 such means the structure of the sublime state is corrupted. The treasury exists through the abundance of the *reaya* . . . the state exists through them and the revenues collected from them.

Everyone in Ottoman society had his place, determined by his occupation and his religion. It was the sultan's function to see that this rigid class structure was maintained, because only in that way would the state organisation operate properly. By the second half of the seventeenth century all writers agreed that this balance of society had been upset:

> 1 . . . the *reaya* no longer obeyed the sultan's commands and soldiers turned against the sultan. There was no respect for the authorities and they were attacked, not by words but by blows. All acted as they pleased. As tyranny and injustice increased,
> 5 people in the provinces began to flee to Istanbul. The old order and harmony are departing. When they have finally collapsed, catastrophe will surely follow.

It was easy enough to see that something had gone wrong with society. To find the causes for this was more difficult.

2 Ottoman Views on the Reasons for Decline

When Ottoman writers attempted to analyse the reasons for the empire's decline, they saw the *symptoms* and mistook them for the underlying causes. They were convinced that it was happening because the tried and trusty ways of earlier times, particularly those of the Golden Age of Suleiman the Magnificent, were not being properly followed. If the corruption and inefficiency which had crept into government administration could be eradicated, the *timar* system revitalised and overhauled, and the sultan's power restored to its former level through enforcement of the traditional social structure, then all would again be well. Nothing new was needed. It was merely a matter of making the traditional arrangements work properly. Changed circumstances and external influences were totally ignored as irrelevant. It was this closed mind which, in the end, frustrated and brought to naught all the Ottoman efforts.

a) The Sultans

In such a centralised and abolutist state as the Ottoman empire, the personality and ability of the sultan was very important. Although it is no longer historically fashionable to put too much stress on the influence of individual rulers or politicians on a country's history, there is no doubt that the sharp decline in the quality of the sultans played a part in the Ottoman troubles of the seventeenth century. Many of them were physically, mentally or emotionally damaged, given to drunkenness, or, as the chronicler delicately expresses it, having 'an unusually strenuous passion for women'. There were exceptions, such as Murad IV, but the majority were incompetent, pleasure loving spendthrifts, who no longer controlled government decisions. After the late sixteenth century it became very unusual for the sultan to accompany the army on campaign, let alone to lead it into battle. More and more, power passed into the hands of the great officials – the Grand Vezirs, the *agas* of the Janissaries, and the *Kizlar agas* (literally the 'commanders of the girls', the Black Eunuchs in charge of the harem) – or the *valide* sultan (the Queen mother). Often the sultan was only a child at his accession, and quickly became the victim of harem intrigues.

These difficulties arose largely because all the seventeenth century sultans came to the throne without having had any experience of government, Murad III (1574–95), was the last sultan to have been trained as a provincial governor, and none of his successors had seen active service with the army before their accession. The old custom of allowing the sultan's sons to fight for the throne with the expectation that the strongest, most able and most intelligent would win, for failure meant certain death, was replaced by an apparently more humane system (selection by seniority). Mehmed III (1595–1603) was the last sultan to follow the Law of Fratricide and to dispose of his brothers. In this case 19 of them were killed, plus a large number of assorted female relatives. To prevent another such orgy of killing, and to ensure that the House of Osman would continue even if the Sultan left not direct heir, it was decided that the brothers and sons of the sultan should be kept prisoners in the 'cage' for the duration of their lives. There they would not be able to foment rebellion against the sultan, but would be available to ascend the throne in order of seniority. By the later seventeenth century, brothers had come to take precedence over sons.

These arrangements led to difficulties. The majority of seventeenth century sultans, brought up in seclusion, with no normal social life and no political or military experience, were totally unfitted to rule. Only too often the eventual successor was old, and psychologically unable to cope with the demands of public life. Contemporary writers did not appreciate this. They merely saw weak sultans, who destroyed the stability of the state by allowing power to fall into the hands of 'irresponsible persons'. They also believed that these 'persons' used the sultan's authority for their own ends, and that bribery and corruption were the result. But bribery at the top had been a perpetual problem since the early sixteenth century. In the 1540s Suleiman's Grand Vezir, Lufti Pasha, had complained, 'Bribes to officials are an incurable disease. O God, save us from bribes!' The situation became worse after the decision by Rustem Pasha to reintroduce the sale of offices. Bribery and corruption, coupled with oppression, spread downwards through the administrative system, reaching epidemic proportions by the seventeenth century.

At his death in 1603 Mehmed III left two teenage sons, Ahmed who succeeded to the throne, and Mustafa. Ahmed was as yet childless, and it was decided to allow Mustafa to live, although, or perhaps because, he was mentally defective. Ahmed I had several sons, but died before any of them were of age. He was succeeded by Mustafa, who quickly proved unsuitable to be sultan, and was removed after three months. He was replaced by Ahmed's son, Osman II, who was assassinated four years later as the result of palace intrigues between his mother and a number of senior officials. This event provided a precedent for the assassination of a reigning sultan. After a brief and equally unsatisfactory second reign by Mustafa, the sultanate passed to Osman's brother, Murad IV. But he left no surviving sons on his death in 1640.

Murad was succeeded by his remaining brother Ibrahim, who had been kept in the 'cage' since childhood, and was mentally disturbed by the sudden change in his life. His mother, Kösem, the *valide* sultan (the queen mother) was persuaded that he should be deposed, and in 1648 this was done. He was later murdered. He was succeeded by his son Mehmed IV, whose reign was to last nearly 40 years.

b) The Sultanate of the Women

Mehmed was only a young child at the time of his accession. Inevitably this led to palace intrigues. His mother, Turhan, attempted to control the government, despite the opposition of her rival, Kösem (the mother of Ibrahim and grandmother of Mehmed). Kösem plotted to replace Mehmed with one of his brothers, but she was murdered on Turhan's orders, before she could put her plan into effect. Turhan became the controlling power behind the child sultan, ushering in the period of Ottoman history known as the 'Sultanate of the Women'.

That strong-minded women of the harem should intrigue on behalf of themselves and their children with the Grand Vezir, the *aga* of the

Janissaries, and other powerful figures was nothing new. Roxelana, Suleiman's wife, had plotted to get rid of the Grand Vezir Ibrahim, and of Suleiman's son, Mustafa. She had also intrigued to further the careers of her son-in-law, Rustem Pasha, and of Mehmed Sokollu, Suleiman's last Grand Vezir. It was she who had the harem removed from their isolation in the old palace to the Topkapi palace, where they would be nearer the centre of government and more in touch with events. The personal and private access which the favoured women of the harem enjoyed, made them a powerful force within the government, especially when the sultan was incompetent or weak. The influence of the *valide* sultan was particularly important when the sultan was a child.

Turhan encouraged her son to indulge his passion for hunting, while she looked after affairs of state. She was assisted by a series of Grand Vezirs, none of whom remained in office very long. They were deposed or executed as the result of in-fighting among competing palace factions. Turhan was quite unable to deal with the problems which arose, including an empty treasury, an armed rebellion and a breakdown of law and order, arising from a corrupt and inefficient administration. Only the appointment of Mehmed Köprülü as Grand Vezir in 1656 saved the sultanate and the empire from disaster.

When Mehmed IV was deposed in 1687 he was succeeded by two of his now elderly brothers, and only on the death of the second one, in 1695, did Mehmed's eldest son become sultan.

c) The Breakdown of the *Timar* System

The *timar* system which provided for tax collection, the maintenance of law and order, the supervision of the *reaya* working the land, and, above all, the provision of armed horsemen, the *sipahis*, for service in the sultan's army, had been the basis of the early and continued military success and sound administration of the Ottoman empire. By the end of the sixteenth century the system was showing signs of strain.

Inflation had begun to affect the *timar* holder. His income was fixed, and the financial problems of the government meant that there was no state money available to supplement his income to meet rising prices. Many *timar* holders could not afford to equip themselves and their horses to go on campaign. As a result their *timar* grants were revoked. Others, unable to make ends meet, simple left their *timars* and migrated to the cities, or joined the growing bands of brigands which roamed the countryside. *Timars* thus left vacant increasingly fell into the hands of Janissaries, palace officials, court favourites, women and members of the *reaya*. Many of the *timar* holders oppressed and exploited the *reaya*, by exacting higher taxes and imposing illegal levies. At the same time they avoided as far as possible fulfilling their military obligations. Many even converted their *timars* into *vakifs* (pious foundations) or, as the sultan's central authority weakened, into private property. The numbers of feudal *sipahis* declined from 87 000 in 1560 to only 8000 in 1610, the *reaya* suffered, justice was not done and public order deteriorated.

The infiltration of the *reaya* into the *askeri* class through the acquisition of *timars* meant a loss of revenue, because they escaped their tax obligations. To the Ottoman mind, even more important, was the fact that by blurring the edges between the two great social divisions, they were imperilling the Circle of Equity.

d) The Janissaries and the end of the *Devshirme*

As the number of *timars* declined and the number of *sipahis* with them, the government began to look elsewhere for its soldiers. In any case, by the seventeenth century, the *sipahis* with their old fashioned bows and arrows, sword and shield were becoming obsolete as a fighting force. They were unwilling to use firearms, which they considered unchivalrous and unbecoming to free cavalry men, although they agreed that guns might be good enough for slave infantry like the Janissaries. As a result, the *sipahis* became increasingly useless in battle against the European armies, with their more sophisticated weapons, particularly their hand guns. The government decided, therefore, to concentrate on building up the *Kapikulu* troops, the sultan's slave army of the Janissaries and the *Sipahis* of the Porte.

In 1527 there were about 8000 Janissaries. By 1627 their numbers had risen to 38 000. The *Sipahis* of the Porte increased from 5000 to close on 21 000 in the same period. At the same time, significant changes were taking place within these two sections of the standing army. These showed that the old order was breaking down. The sultan's army was no longer being recruited solely from the *devshirme* (the slaves gathered as tribute from Christian families of the Balkans), or from those taken as prisoners-of-war or bought in the slave markets. The *devshirme* had become unsatisfactory. It was a question of supply and demand. In the fifteenth and sixteenth centuries new territories in the Balkans were being conquered, and these provided large numbers of potential pages and Janissaries. As the empire ceased to expand, it became more and more difficult to find suitable children in areas which had already been heavily exploited. In addition, fewer successful wars meant too that fewer prisoners were available to the slave system. This, at a time when the Janissary corps was being expanded and the bureaucracy staffing increased, meant that the *devshirme* was no longer viable. It was finally abolished in the mid-seventeenth century, during the reign of Mehmed IV. It had ceased to fulfil its function because it could no longer provide enough recruits; it was necessary to look for other sources of supply.

In a radical change of policy, in future, only those born Moslem, and therefore free, were recruited into the army. But this simply regularised what had increasingly been the situation for a long time, the infiltration of the army by freeborn Moslems. Many of these were the sons of Janissaries, who were, by the reign of Suleiman, allowed to marry. The government had long held out against the enrolment of Janissaries' sons, who were Moslem and free, but with the end of the *devshirme* had no choice but to give way. The need to build up the numbers of Janissaries meant that it was not long before members of the *reaya*, who were also Moslem and free, were allowed to enrol. This was a further disruption of the Circle of Equity, by the admission of members of the *reaya* into the *askeri* class.

The Janissaries had been a very important part of the strength of the Ottoman empire. They were trained and disciplined men whose sole aim was to serve the sultan, and, if necessary, to die for him. They had had no family commitments and no other distractions. However, once they were allowed to marry, their attitudes changed. They began to put the welfare of their families first. They were less willing to go on lengthy or dangerous campaigns away from home, or to live the harsh regimented and communal life previously expected of them. Many acquired their own houses in the capital or in the other towns in which they were garrisoned, instead of living in barracks. In peace time they occupied themselves with civilian trades or commercial enterprises, so that they were more like a part-time militia than a standing army. They became rich and powerful, arrogant and corrupt. Discipline was slack, and the men even more difficult to control than before. While they still showed personal bravery in war, their training in general was less thorough and their overall military performance was much less impressive.

To maintain these ever growing numbers of soldiers put a great financial strain on the government. The demands of the Janissaries for money increased every year. Their pay, due every three months, frequently fell into arrears early in the seventeenth century, when financial difficulties began to affect the government. Late payments were often made in debased coinage. This really amounted to a reduction in pay, and led to riots and uprisings, especially in Istanbul. The long established custom of a new sultan making an 'accession gift' of money to each Janissary, turned into demands by the men for larger and larger sums of money as of right on these occasions. There were even occasions on which the Janissaries were influential in deposing or otherwise disposing of a sultan, in order to obtain a 'donation' from his successor. To find all this money for the Janissaries meant more and heavier taxes being imposed on the *reaya*. This led in turn to social disturbances throughout the empire.

e) *Sekbans* and the *Jelali* Riots

The *Jelali* Riots arose mainly from the Ottoman government's military policy at the end of the sixteenth century. A contributory factor was the growing number of landless peasants (*sekbans*) who had no work and no settled home, and who turned to banditry (see below). At the time of the 'Long War' against Hungary (1593–1606), the Ottomans faced large Austrian armies equipped with muskets. In 1602 the Ottoman commander appealed to the sultan, 'In field or siege we are in a distressed position, because most enemy forces are infantry armed with muskets, while most of ours are horsemen (feudal *sipahis*) and we have few skilled with muskets.' As a result of this plea, the sultan ordered *sekbans* (landless youths from the *reaya*) to be collected from all over the Balkans and Anatolia, and hired for short-term duty as musketeers. They were enrolled in companies of either infantry or cavalry, and were paid from revenues collected from vacant *timars*. Some provincial governors enrolled their own companies of *sekbans*, and these were paid for by yet further taxes on the peasants.

This decision to enlist the *reaya* was in direct contravention of the Ottoman regulation that the *reaya* should not be allowed weapons of any kind, and especially not firearms. Government documents of the time show, however, that most of the *reaya* already either owned, or had access to a musket. The manufacture and import of arms was a state monopoly, with severe penalties for illegal possession, but smuggled guns were plentiful and cheap, and home-made ones common. By enrolling the *sekbans* the government was simply accepting, and making use of, an existing if illegal state of affairs, which it appeared powerless to control. Better to regularise the *reaya's* possession of firearms and channel their use to official advantage. This worked well during the war and the *sekbans* fought bravely.

At the end of the campaign they were paid off and sent home. In Anatolia, especially, they could find no work, and most joined local rebel gangs, who were already roaming the countryside, robbing and looting. These groups, the *jelalis*, terrorised Anatolia between 1595 and 1610, resulting in a mass migration by peasant refugees from the area, and known in Ottoman history as 'the great flight'. The sultan's authority was ignored. His army was powerless against the *jelali* leaders, who could bring 20000 armed men into battle, and were well able to take on the best of the Janissaries. Only by an all-out effort, and by sheer weight of numbers were the sultan's troops able to subdue the rebels. Afterwards, in true Ottoman tradition, thousands of rebels were executed as a warning to others, so that the commander of the sultan's army became known as 'the well-digger', an allusion to the mass graves dug for the multitudes who had been executed.

Companies of Janissaries and *Sipahis* of the Porte were stationed in the provincial towns of Anatolia to complete the pacification programme. They soon married into the local families, engaged in trade and commerce, grew extremely rich and became the dominant power in the area, where they eventually completely supplanted the authority of the central government.

3 Causes of Decline

Ottoman writers concentrated on the disruption of the Circle of Equity as the main reason for the decline of the empire. They argued that this disruption was brought about through the loss of central authority by weak sultans, by the breakup of the *timar* system, and by the ending of the *devshirme*, all of which affected the military power of the empire, as well as its economic and social stability.

However, there were other deeper and more complex causes. These were not understood by the Ottomans, and, in any case, were largely beyond their control.

a) Population Explosion

There was an enormous growth in population within the empire, especially in Anatolia. Census research by Turkish historians indicates a probable population for the empire of some 12 or 13 million in 1525, rising to 17 or 18 million by 1580 and to as much as 25 or 30 million by 1600.

In the early days of the empire, in the full flower of conquest, there was more land available than could easily be worked by the existing population. Resettlement programmes and strict enforcement of the *reaya's* obligations to remain on the land and cultivate it, gradually brought all suitable land into agricultural use. With the virtual end of conquests, population increases outstripped the amount of land available for cultivation. Many holdings could no longer support the number of dependents now living on them, and many young peasants had to find a living elsewhere. Some were hired by the government as *sekbans*, during wartime, but they presented a serious problem to the government in time of peace. A number of them joined up with existing bandits from nomadic Anatolian tribes, as at the time of the *Jelali* riots. They ravaged the countryside in search of a living, defying the sultan's authority, and contributing to a breakdown of law and order. Some who did not become bandits, broke their legal obligations to remain on the land and fled to the town. Whether or not they were successful in finding employment, and most, being unskilled, did not, they represented a financial loss to the state, because there they were not subject to taxation. These challenges to the sultan's authority were recognised by Ottoman writers at the time, but the underlying cause, that of population increases and accompanying shortage of agricultural land, escaped them.

b) Inflation

State income came mainly from revenues raised from agricultural land, the *timars*, and depended on a continuing stable currency. The income available from the land was finite (there was only so much land, and by the seventeenth century the limits of production had been reached). Any devaluation of the currency would necessitate heavy increases in taxation to make good the shortfall in state income. Any increase in taxation would lead to oppression of the *reaya* and social disturbances. The sixteenth-century price rises affected the empire as much as the west. Turkish historians have made a study of the cost of individual commodities, which show that in the 50 years between the death of Suleiman and 1616, prices rose sharply. The prices of some goods, such as grain, butter, oil and salt doubled or trebled. Other foodstuffs showed even greater rises, among them honey, the standard sweetener used in cooking. The reason for the sudden and severe 'price revolution' in Europe is generally ascribed to the influx of precious metals from South America. While other factors may have been involved, such as the increase in population outstripping food production, and prices being forced up by scarcity, it appears to be true to say that the main cause of inflation in the Ottoman empire was the cheap silver, mainly from Peru, entering the empire via Ragusa (Dubrovnik) and Genoa. The Ottoman economy, which was based on a silver coinage was particularly vulnerable to this flood of imported silver.

At the same time the government faced, not only enormous expenses in connection with long wars first against Persia and then against Austria, but also the mounting costs of maintaining an expanding army and a growing bureaucracy. Several ways to reduce the effects of inflation were tried. In 1584 the coinage was debased, reducing the silver content by 40%. This brought short-term relief and substantial quick profits for the government, but the long-term results were catastrophic. The Ottoman coinage lost value against other European currencies and became increasingly unacceptable to foreign traders, even in the internal markets of the empire. Faced with a depreciating coinage, the government was forced to increase taxation to meet expenses. This placed additional burdens on the tax-paying peasants, who were already suffering from the price rise, and led to more unrest.

Attempts were made to raise money in other ways. Estates of exiled or executed officials were seized and converted to government use, and the practice of tax farming extended. Although the poll-tax, payable by non-Moslem subjects, increased sixfold between 1560 and 1600, and doubled again by the 1650s, and special emergency taxes, used only rarely in the past, were converted into annual taxes on all subjects, it was still not enough. The treasury remained permanently in deficit.

The Ottomans were aware of these effects, but they did not clearly understand their causes. Nor could they find ways of dealing with them. Nor, too, did they realise that the problem of inflation was one of the factors disrupting the Circle of Equity.

c) The End of Conquests

This has to be one of the main causes of Ottoman decline. As early as 1560 the age of conquest was drawing to a close. Only two more important acquisitions were to be made in the west, Cyprus in 1570 and Crete a century later in 1669. In the east substantial territorial gains were made against Persia, but they could not be held for long. By 1700 the empire was beginning to shrink.

The Ottoman state had been founded on conquest and had been maintained by further conquests. These provided the land for *timars* and for cultivation, wealth from taxes paid by the *reaya* working these lands, candiates for the *devshirme*, employment for central and provincial government officials and for members of the *ulema*, and initially, of course, large quantities of booty. Troublesome elements in the population at home could be provided with suitable occupation. They either migrated of their own accord into the frontier areas, attracted by financial rewards offered by service there, or were uprooted and forcibly resettled in desolate parts of the new lands.

When new lands were no longer available, no new *timars* could be granted, and applicants were forced to wait for vacancies brought about by the death of existing holders – often a long wait. The number of new posts available for members of the *ulema*, either as teachers in the mosques or as part of the judiciary, was also reduced, causing serious unrest among students in the religious colleges, which had over-expanded, confident that vacancies to fill would continue indefinitely. Many of these unemployed students joined the disaffected groups of peasants already terrorising town and countryside.

Devshirme levies became more difficult to raise, and the system was finally abandoned (see page 122). No longer was it true that

1 If a man seriously considers the whole composition of the Turkish court, he will find it to be a prison of slaves, differing from that where the galley slaves are immured only by the ornaments and glittering outside.

Why did the Conquests End?
*Constraints imposed by the empire's geographical and logistical limitations was one reason. The choice of Istanbul as the capital fixed the limitations of Ottoman expansion. The capital was the centre of government, and the army needed to be quartered nearby. To transport it, and its equipment and supplies on campaign required tens of thousands of oxen, camels and horses. The *sipahis* brought their own transport, but, because of the weather, they could not set out before the

end of winter in late April, and had to be sent home before the end of October, to collect their revenues and see to their crops and animals. The whole army, about 100000 men, would take up to two or three months to arrive at the front, whether in the east or west, and as long again to travel back, leaving a campaining season of only six or eight weeks. The furthest limits which could be reached, therefore, in a summer campaign were Vienna in the west and Tabriz in the east. Any longer journey and there would have been no time for fighting, before it was time to return home. Although it was possible on occasion for the army to winter in Persia, this was never the case in the Balkans, where the weather was too severe.

In the early days of the empire, as the Ottomans advanced, so did the capital, to keep up with the new frontier, moving from Bursa to Edirne before Mehmed the Conqueror made Istanbul his permanent capital. He was attracted to the city by its Byzantine and Roman imperial traditions, of which he saw himself as the inheritor in 1453. Istanbul seemed to him to have certain special advantages. It had a great natural harbour, the Golden Horn, complete with large dockyards; and the city was strategically placed. It was the bridge between Europe and Asia. It was almost in the centre of his existing empire, all the frontiers of which were then within easy striking distance of the city. The choice of Istanbul as the capital did not, therefore, at first, seem to impose any limitation to expansion.

The limitation, when it came, was twofold. By the middle of the sixteenth century, Istanbul had become the permanent political and military base of the empire, even though it proved by then to be too far from the new frontiers to allow easy campaigning there. The city which Mehmed and his successors rebuilt and beautified, with the great mosques which still dominate the skyline, symbolises an Ottoman turning away from frontier warfare and expansion towards the foundation of a stable High Islamic empire based around their newly acquired historic capital. This aspect was reinforced once the Holy Cities of Mecca and Medina came under Ottoman protection, and the sultan became the Caliph and Champion of Islam. The Ottomans were further committed to remaining in Istanbul, for even if they had wished to move the capital into the Balkans to make westward expansion possible, it could not have been done. It would have meant leaving Mecca and Medina unprotected against attack, not just from non-Moslems, such as the Portuguese, but fellow Moslems, such as the Shi'ite followers of the Safavid shahs of Persia. Equally they could not move the capital further east without leaving the Balkans unprotected. Istanbul was to remain the capital of the empire until 1923.

Another reason for the end of Ottoman conquests, was the failure of the Ottomans to keep up with advances in European military technology and tactics. The Ottomans had first come across cannon in the late fourteenth century in the course of their Balkan campaigns. They had been using them as siege guns, firing large stone balls to knock down city walls, since the 1420s. These guns were large and unwieldy, and so difficult to transport, that they were usually cast on the spot, outside the walls of the fortress or city. By 1456 Mehmed the Conqueror had the most powerful artillery in Europe, evoking 'admiration and disbelief amongst all those who saw it' outside Belgrade.

Early in the fifteenth century small cannon (bombards) about 18″ long were being made in Europe, and being exported to the Ottoman empire. These were the first handguns and foreshadowed the arquebus and the later musket, with which Suleiman tried to arm the Janissaries. There are continual references in Ottoman sources to their soldiers' unwillingness to use firearms, and to the efficient use of them by the enemy. In 1529, 'great losses' were caused by the Austrian infantry's muskets, while de Busbecq comments in 1555 that 'our pistols and carbines, which are used on horseback, are a great terror to the Turks'. Fifteen years later the Grand Vezir, Rustem Pasha was trying to arm 200 *sipahis* of the Porte with pistols. He failed because 'Turks are against this armature, because it is slovenly (for they are much for cleanness in war) for the troopers' hands are made black and sooty and their clothes full of spots.'

In battle the Ottoman usually advanced their cavalry in a pincer movement. designed to cut off the advancing enemy centre (as they did at Mohaçs), but they generally preferred to follow an advance with a simulated retreat intended to lure the pursuing enemy headlong into a trap laid by the Janissaries. Their tactics had changed very little by the late seventeenth century. So had their equipment, although firearms had become rather more general. However, their European enemies' tactics and equipment had changed radically between 1560 and 1700. New formations of pikemen were used to defeat any possible Ottoman pincer movement, and cuirassiers (cavalry with defensive armour) were employed as shock troops to break up the Janissary formations. In the 1680s pikes became obsolete, and were replaced by *chevaux de frise* and bayonets, as well as faster-firing and more accurate guns. New battle-square troop formations came into use too.

In 1596 an Ottoman historian had lamented that the enemy, by using modern weapons, had gained an advantage and urged the Ottoman commanders to protect their soldiers by equipping them with the same weapons. This was a course of action which, throughout the seventeenth century, the Ottomans showed themselves incapable of taking. They could not accept that the arms and tactics employed by Suleiman, which had brought such a splendid series of military successes, were no longer effective. Circumstances had changed. The Ottomans had not, and military defeat in Europe was inevitable. In 1683 and 1697 the Ottoman army was cut to pieces.

d) Ottoman Conservatism

Although the Ottomans in the early years of the fifteenth century had been sufficiently receptive to outside ideas to adopt the use of cannon, this attitude changed dramatically. As the empire ceased to expand, land frontiers in the Balkans hardened and stabilised. The empire became inward looking. Change was anathema, particularly in anything affected by the *sheriat*. Any deviation from the Sunnite teachings, the orthodox way of the Prophet, was unthinkable. The heretical Shi'ites were regarded with the same horror as Christians, perhaps more so. Suleiman's Grand Vezir Rustem Pasha told de Busbecq, 'I assure you we abhor the Persians, and regard them as more unholy than we regard you Christians.'

For the Ottomans, Moslem superiority over all other faiths and all other modes of life was a certainty. Therefore, the rest of the world had nothing of value to communicate, and was best ignored. The Islamic year 1000 (1591–2), when Moslems expected the world to end, passed without incident. This confirmed the Ottomans in their belief that God was pleased with them, and they their empire had reached the highest pinnacle of perfection possible for any Islamic state. The Ottomans had the comfortable certainty that they were right, and that Europe was wrong. Coming as this did, at a time of great technological and scientific developments in Europe, the Ottomans' rigid adherence to tradition, coupled with their closed minds, led inevitably to a widening of the gap between Europe and the empire, to the grave detriment of the latter.

4 Advice on Reform from Contemporary Ottoman Writers

Many Ottoman historians, officials, judges and men of letters devoted a great deal of effort to discovering what was wrong with the state. They wrote numerous books, letters and memoranda to inform and guide those in authority in general, and the sultan in particular. The authors were intelligent and anxious to be helpful, but were hampered by the tenets of High Islam, which bound them to the Circle of Equity hypothesis and restricted their suggestions for action almost entirely to the traditional 'change nothing, return to the past' approach.

Given that contemporary writers did not appreciate the underlying causes (population increases, inflation, end of conquests, resistance to change) of the empire's troubles, was the advice they gave realistic? Could it be put into practice? And if so, did it work?

'Letters of Advice' were being drawn up and submitted to the sultan from the mid-sixteenth century onwards. Already in the reign of Suleiman the Magnificent there was disquiet about corruption and inefficiency in the administration, which the Grand Vezir Lufti Pasha embodied in the first known 'Letter of Advice'. He wrote that the wise minister must be without greed or private interests, and must persuade the sultan to act justly to protect the rights of his subjects. The Grand Vezir must be honest in his dealings with the sultan and must not take bribes. Appointments must be made only on merit, and all complaints against officials must be carefully investigated. Taxes must be correctly and fairly collected and supplementary taxes should be abolished. Otherwise the overburdered *reaya* would abandon their land and flee to the towns (where they would not have to pay taxes). If this happened, the financial stability of the empire would be wrecked.

None of these points was new, and the whole was in fact a plea for a return to the good old days. This was to be echoed in Letter after Letter in reign after reign in the next 150 years. But this does not mean that nothing was done. The frequently expressed idea of western historians that the sultans neither listened to advice, nor made any efforts to halt the decline, is wrong. There were a number of occasions on which the sultan tried to revitalise the empire.

a) Attempts at Reform

*One Sultan, Osman II (1618–22), did try to make radical changes in the whole Ottoman state system. He distrusted, as a corrupting influence, the appointment of senior officials from among the converted Christians of the *devshirme* and believed that there was a need to 'Turkify' the palace and the army. He wanted to replace the Janissaries with a national militia of Moslem Anatolian peasants, and to move the capital from Istanbul back into Anatolia, either to Ankara or Bursa. The Janissaries, already upset by a miserly 'accession donation', and by the Sultan's, not unjustified, criticism of their military discipline, held meetings to protest against the Sultan's plan to dissolve the Corps. Words soon gave place to action: the palace was attacked, Osman was seized and afterwards assassinated. All that Osman had achieved was to provide a precedent for the assassination of a ruling sultan, and to increase the power of the Janissaries to decide affairs of state. No other sultan ever again tried to carry out such far reaching changes, or to act in such an independent manner. Ottoman conservatism had triumphed.

This conservatism was to find expression in the writings of Mustafa Kochu Bey, when, in 1631, he presented his *'Treatise on Government'* to Murad IV. This laid the foundations of the traditional reform movement, from which no future sultan was ever to depart. This movement was the attempt to remedy present troubles by a return to past practice. But it was increasingly a past seen through a nostalgic haze, a Golden Age which never was, or at least never was in the way in which it was perceived in the seventeenth century. The reign of Suleiman the Magnificent was held up as a time of high moral standards, and impeccable behaviour in public life, when every man knew his place and kept it in a stable society. The evidence of Lufti Pasha to the contrary was conveniently ignored.

In his Treatise Mustafa Kochu rehearsed the signs of decline and deplored the sultan's loss of power, the increase of conflicts and intrigues within the harem and among palace officials, the oppression of the *reaya* and their flight to the towns, with consequent loss of revenue, and the financial corruption and military inefficiency throughout the empire. Firm and decisive action by the sultan was necessary to put the state back on the right lines. Murad IV conscientiously tried to follow this advice.

*At the beginning of his reign Murad was only 13. It was a time of political unrest and financial disaster. The Grand Vezir could only maintain his position by bribing the army with money in the form of coins made by melting down gold and silver objects from the palace. When he was dismissed by the Sultan, and this source of income was lost to the soldiers, there were military uprisings both in Anatolia and in Rumelia. The next Grand Vezir foolishly advised that the best way to bring the risings under control, was to summon all Janissaries and *sipahis* of the Porte to Istanbul to state their grievances. Thousands of undisciplined soldiers ran wild in the streets of the capital. Outside the palace gates they literally tore apart 17 leading government officials who were unfortunate enough to fall into their hands. The Janissaries then forced the Sultan to appoint a Grand Vezir of their choosing under whom matters became even worse. Taxes were raised, the coinage was debased, and gangs of lawless soldiers and peasants roamed about town and countryside, looting and killing. With extreme difficulty, Murad IV, the only courageous and able sultan of the seventeenth century, managed to reassert his authority. When he came of age, he dismissed the Grand Vezir and forced all members of the *askeri* class (which included all members of the government and the army) to take a personal oath of loyalty to himself. Order was restored. Murad then set out to save the empire, as Kochu Bey had suggested, not by introducing changes, but by making the old institutions work.

He reformed and reorganised the *timar* system, which for a while, again became the financial and political basis for a strong army and sound administration. Any *sipahis* unable or unwilling to perform their military duties were dismissed and their holdings were given to Janissaries. Bribery and corruption among officials were largely eliminated, and justice was enforced. Particular efforts were made to protect the *reaya* from oppression. Attempts were made to restore moral standards by strict enforcement of Islamic law. Murad was greatly helped in this campaign by a fire which destroyed a quarter of Istanbul, including 2000 buildings, the Janissaries' barracks and all the government archives. He called the disaster a sign from God of his displeasure, and used it to bolster up his campaign for purity and austerity. The use of coffee and tobacco was prohibited, and the wearing of elaborate or luxurious dress forbidden. A network of spies was set up to enforce the regulations, and Murad himself roamed the streets, personally executing wrongdoers. A system of censorship prevented free speech, and many public figures met sudden and unexplained deaths. It is not surprising that Murad became one of the most unpopular sultans. He was also one of the richest, due to his efficient re-organisation of the tax system. As a Venetian said, what Murad did he did for cash, not for law, justice or prayer. His full treasury enabled him to pay the army and to keep their allegiance. This ensured his own safety, and allowed him to do as he wished. No sultan had exercised the same power since Suleiman. He died in 1641, at the age of 30, having 'by force of personality, and by executing 20 000 men, brought some stability and restored much of the empire's vigour.'

Evliya Chelebi (see page 148) was a page in the palace from 1636 to 1638, and became, according to his own account, a close friend of Murad, with whom he was almost of an age, and with whom he shared a fondness for jokes. Even he, though, was not blind to Murad's faults:

1 He was brave and intelligent, with immense physical strength and
  energy, excelling at wrestling, boxing and throwing the javelin.
  His fingers were thick but well proportioned and the most
  powerful wrestler could not open his clenched fist. He usually
5 dressed in blue silk, and liked to ride very fast. The Ottoman
  dynasty never produced a prince so athletic, so well built, so
  despotic, so dreaded of his foes or so majestic. Cruel and
  bloodthirsty as he was, he was fond of conversing with rich and
10 poor alike . . . No other monarch, however, perpetrated so many
  acts of cruelty. So carefully did he watch over the Ottoman
  dominions that no bird flew over without him knowing it. But
  were we to describe all his excellent qualities, we should fill yet
15 another volume.

But Murad's reforms could not put the clock back, and they gave only a temporary respite brought about by repressive force in the hands of a strong sultan. The following reign, that of Ibrahim the Mad, 'so manifested and magnified the ills of the state that no Ottoman ruler ever again took that name, or gave it to his children'. He left an empty treasury, a restive army, a corrupt government and a poverty-stricken land for his successor.

* In 1656, in his *Guide to Practice for the Rectification of Defects*, Katip Chelebi repeated to the new sultan, Mehmed IV, the warnings of Kochu Bey. Ketip Chelebi's political theory was based on the idea that a state passes through three stages – first vigorous developments, followed by a stationary peak, and then a slow decline. He believed that the empire was about to enter the third stage, but that it could be prevented from doing so. He explained how in the first stage the state

protected the peasants from oppression, so that they cultivated the land well, and could pay high taxes. In this situation everyone prospered. In the second stage overtaxation led to social disturbances, during which peasants left the land. The countryside was uncultivated, while the towns became overcrowded. He attributed much of this trouble to the giving of bribes (*bakshish*) to government officials by people wanting jobs, so that money which should have gone to the Treasury was finding its way into the pockets of individuals. As a result the Treasury was in debt, and had to increase the general level of taxation paid by the peasants in order to make ends meet. He recommended that there should be an end to the sale of offices, that a just taxation system should be re-established, and that existing laws should be universally enforced. The efficiency of the army must be restored, but, in view of the serious financial situation, it must be reduced to a more realistic size in order to balance the budget.

5 The Köprülü Era

The strong and honest leadership, advocated by Katip Chelebi, was provided for the whole of the second half of the seventeenth century by the very remarkable Köprülü family. As successive Grand Vezirs, they took over in all but name the role of the sultan, and tried to put into practice the advice given by Katip Chelebi and his predecessor, Kochu Bey.

Mehmed Köprülü, the first member of the family to take office, was well into his eighties when he was appointed Grand Vezir by Mehmed IV in 1656. There had not been a capable and efficient Grand Vezir for nearly a century, and at first it seemed unlikely that Köprülü would be any different from his immediate predecessors. He had been born in the 1570s, probably in Albania, and had been one of the *devshirme* youths. When he left the palace service, he received the grant of a *timar* in Anatolia, having first been a Janissary and then a treasury official. In his sixties he was fortunate to find a patron in Murad IV's last and most capable Grand Vezir. He was appointed by him to various important posts in the provinces, including Trebizond where he learnt much about the causes of popular unrest and dissatisfaction. He gained the reputation of being an honest and able administrator.

Mehmed Köprülü accepted the position of Grand Vezir only on his own terms. The Sultan was not to make any decrees with which the Grand Vezir did not agree, and was not to listen to any malicious stories about him. In addition, all government appointments and dismissals were to be made by the Grand Vezir and not by the Sultan. These provisions gave Köprülü greater power than any Grand Vezir before him, even greater than the power of Ibrahim and Rustem Pasha in the days of Suleiman the Magnificent. This was especially so after he moved the seat of government from the Sultan's palace to his own house. As a result the old imperial council, the *Divan*, lost all its former importance.

Mehmed Köprülü was the answer to Katip Chelebi's prayer that 'a man of the sword' (that is, a man of action), not 'a man of the pen' (a bureaucrat) might appear and save the empire. He reintroduced many of the reforms of Murad IV, balanced the budget by reducing the excessive size of the army, and managed to restore a measure of prosperity to the hard pressed *reaya*.

He was succeeded by other members of his family, who further increased the power of the Grand Vezir. Under their guidance, the empire recovered sufficient military and economic strength to mount the second great attack on Vienna in 1683. Although the current Köprülü Grand Vezir was blamed for the army's failure to take the city, and was executed, the family continued to guide the fortunes of the empire into the early years of the next century. The army was reformed and remodelled after the Vienna debacle, a new coinage was issued to replace the old debased one, and a fairer system of taxation was introduced. By 1690 reasonable success was achieved even in stamping out corruption. About this time the most famous of all the Ottoman historians, Mustafa Naima Effendi, arrived in Istanbul.

a) Naima's advice

*Naima had been born in Aleppo around 1665, the son and grandson of Janissary officers, who had made money trading in that city. In Istanbul he trained as a scribe, and was appointed to a senior government position. He came eventually into the service of yet another Köprülü, Hussein, who became Grand Vezir in 1699.

Hussein Köprülü, the greatest reformer the Ottoman empire was ever to have, needed a spokesman to make the humiliating treaty of Karlowitz acceptable to the people. He found that advocate in Naima, who defended Hussein's policies most eloquently, drawing a parallel with the actions of the Prophet Mohammed, who had once had to make an unpopular but necessary peace treaty. In his book, *The Garden of Hussein, being the Choicest of News of the East and West*, Naima referred to the story, 'showing how important it is to make armistices with infidel kings, so that the domains may be put in order and the population have rest.'

Naima's analysis of the situation in 1699 drew upon the ideas of Katip Chelebi. It was based on the familiar Islamic model, likening the state to the human body and the Grand Vezir to the doctor. The state, like the body, goes through stages of birth, growth and decay. Treatment for ills of the state, as for those of the body, was to diagnose, treat and restore to health. Naima extended these ideas. He wrote of the five stages in the life of the Ottoman state; the 'heroic' period of establishment; the period of consolidation under the House of Osman and its slave officials; the period of security and tranquillity; the period of contentment and surfeit, and, finally, the period of disintegration and dissipation. He believed that the empire had entered the fourth stage (contentment and surfeit) about the time of the second siege of Vienna in 1683, and that his patron, Hussein Köprülü, was destined to rouse the empire from its lassitude, and prevent it from slipping into the fifth and final stage.

He went on to suggest five ways in which Hussein could save the empire. He should ensure that the budget balanced; that salaries were paid on time to prevent unrest; that the army was brought up to standard, able to defeat the enemy abroad and maintain peace at home; that the provinces were justly administered so that the reaya could again be prosperous and pay the taxes needed by the government; and that the Sultan should appear cheerful, as this would give his subjects peace of mind.

*Hussein followed Naima's suggestions. In only three years he carried through an ambitious programme of reforms, which tried for the first time since the reign of Suleiman the Magnificent to meet the needs of the peasants as well as of the ruling class. His policy was based on efficient and just government, and on finding economic and financial solutions to the empire's problems. Taxes were geared to the ability to pay, and tax concessions were given to cultivators who returned to their fields. Efforts were made to develop factories to compete with imported European manufactured goods, while excise duties were imposed on imported tobacco, coffee, oil and soap. The army was modernised. Part-time service by the Janissaries was abolished, and the feudal *sipahis* were revitalised by the addition of fully trained nomadic tribesmen from Anatolia. At last an attempt was made to bring the navy up to date, and oared galleys gave way to sailing galleons on the European model. Sailors were properly trained and paid. There were also reforms in the palace and civil service. Incompetent officials were compulsorily retired. An efficiency drive was launched and, for the first time, official documents were dated and copies kept. Unfortunately, no evidence is available about the cheerfulness or otherwise of the Sultan's appearance!

b) Did the Köprülü Reforms Work?

There is no doubt that the Köprülü family, Grand Vezirs for half a century, arrested the deterioration of the Ottoman empire, and left the body politic in better health than at any time since the mid-sixteenth century. Even the disasters of the Vienna campaign and the military defeats leading up to the Treaty of Karlowitz were used as a springboard for further reforms by the tireless Köprülüs.

However, historians disagree about the extent to which the reforms were long lasting. Western historians point to the peasant disturbances in Anatolia around the turn of the century, the Janissary uprisings, and in 1703 the forced abdication of the Sultan, as well as a resurgence of opposition to change among members of the *ulema*, now headed by a new and ambitious *mufti* who had already brought about the resignation and death of Hüseyn Köprülü in 1702. Attention has been drawn to the Treaty of Karlowitz as a decisive turning point in Ottoman history, after which the empire was on the defensive. It has been seen to have been followed by serious internal disorders, the breakdown of local administration and a rapid increase in brigandage in the Balkans, coupled with military weakness, and economic difficulties brought about by changes in trading patterns. Ottoman confidence was destroyed by unaccustomed military defeats and the consequent loss of territory, so that they began to question whether God had abandoned them. Any proposed changes were quickly opposed by the Janissaries and the *ulema*, leading inevitably to further military defeats. No strong sultan emerged to put matters right, so that the decline was resumed.

This view is in contrast with that of Norman Itzkowitz, the American specialist in Turkish history, who believes that Karlowitz was simply a temporary setback, largely overcome by Hüseyn Köprülü's reform programme. In his view the Ottoman army was extremely successful in the early years of the eighteenth century, defeating Peter the Great of Russia in 1711, and regaining the Morea from the Venetians in 1715. Between 1736 and 1739 they defeated the Russians and the Austrians, from whom they recovered Belgrade after threatening an attack on Vienna. After all, as the Ottoman commander told the Austrians, his troops knew the way there! Itzkowitz also points out the great cultural achievements of these years. Known as the 'Tulip Period', it was a time of splendid architectural developments and new advances in the decorative arts. Poetry and literature were encouraged by the introduction of printing into the empire, and musicians and singers were employed in great numbers to entertain at the brilliant and luxurious court festivities. This view is altogether more optimistic than that of the majority of western historians.

6 The Decline – was it rapid, continuous and inevitable?

Despite the traditional belief of the west, the Ottoman decline was none of these things. Fernand Braudel points out in his *Mediterranean World* that it is necessary to look closely at their rate of growth when discussing the rise and fall of empires. It is easy to telescope time and to see not only the signs of greatness but also the signs of decline too early, 'predicting prematurely the collapse of an empire which we know will one day cease to be'. Ottoman decline was not particularly rapid, and was certainly not continuous, being interrupted with varying degrees of success by a series of revivals.

Whether it was inevitable is a more important and significant consideration. Were there inbuilt weaknesses in the system, which, as is often suggested, must lead to eventual decline. Even Braudel wrote of the Ottoman empire showing signs of 'its inexorable decline' by 1600. Certainly, much depended on the strength and ability of the head of the state, the sultan, as must always be the case in an absolutist state. Then the sultan was weak and incompetent, as so often happened during the seventeenth century, the whole empire suffered. The entire Ottoman system was based on continuing war and conquest. When that came to an end, the system could not easily be adapted to function in a more peaceful atmosphere, without losing its religious *raison d'etre*. Changes could have been made to meet new circumstances, but the extreme conservative attitude of mind of the Ottomans made this impossible. In the end it was this inability to accept the need for, or desirability of, change which sealed the fate of the empire.

As for the question of decline – is it just the obvious loss of military power, the end of victory over the enemy, and consequent reduction of territory, or is it an internal breakdown, with economic, social and political difficulties at home, accompanied by widespread bribery, corruption, injustice and oppression. In the eyes of the west, Suleiman was the Magnificent almost entirely because he was the great and successful military commander. It was a title never used by Suleiman's chancery in any document. In the eyes of his people, Suleiman was the Law giver, the purveyor of justice and the embodiment of authority. Does this suggest different views of what made Suleiman's reign the high watermark of Ottoman history? Perhaps at times east and west may have different ideas of what constitutes greatness. Do they also have different ideas of what constitutes decline?

a) Modern Turkish views

*That this may be the case is brought out by the work of Metin Kunt, a Turkish historian, who has researched extensively the changes in provincial administration between 1560 and 1660. He puts forward a totally new idea. He describes how the 'downgrading' of the provincial administrative career had resulted, by 1630, in the appointment of palace and central government officials directly to the top provincial posts as *beylerbeys*, even if they had no previous experience of provincial administration. This was partly due to the fact that central government was becoming more interested in the collection of cash contributions from the provinces than in the maintenance of the increasingly useless feudal *sipahis*. So the *beylerbey* was appointed more as 'overseer of revenues' (tax collector in chief), than as governor of a province. Kunt differs from other historians in believing that this change of emphasis in the duties of the provincial governor, together with the breakdown of the *timar* system, should not be regarded as a 'decline', but as a 'modernisation', in the sense of a shift from a 'feudal' to a 'monetary' system.

To talk of an Ottoman 'decline' from 1600 for the next 300 years or more is, he believes, to follow 'the fallacious notion of a long, monotonous and continuous decline.' It can be argued that where new arrangements, such as the revised duties of the *beylerbey* are introduced, the system is adapting and developing, not declining. The death of an old system is not a 'decline' if it is replaced by something which is better adapted to the needs of the time.

Not all Turkish historians would agree with Kunt, however. Halil Inalcik believes that from the late sixteenth century onwards, 'Ottoman history is the record of decayed forms of ancient imperial institutions; or more correctly of a near eastern state's attempt to adapt to European economic, political and cultural challenge ... (which) made the Ottomans aware that the traditions of a near eastern state had outlived their usefulness.' There is no suggestion here of 'modernisation' to meet changing circumstances.

Western historians have given much more time and effort to the study of the Ottoman empire of the fifteenth and sixteenth centuries than to that of the seventeenth century. This is understandable. The reigns of the colourful, successful sultans like Mehmed the Conqueror and Suleiman the Magnificent, are better documented, at least as far as the west is concerned, than those of the weak failures like Mehmed IV, or the megalomanic Murad IV. For western historians too Ottoman conquests in the Balkans, their continuing threat to central Europe and their naval activities in the Mediterranean bring the Ottomans into the main stream of European history, and make them 'important'. As the threat of further expansion fades, the Ottomans become of less concern, and are simply said to have 'declined'. The decline is almost always seen in terms of military defeat and loss of international prestige. Little or no attention is paid to changes inside the empire. But these developments, some within the Ottomans' control (succession to the sultanate, resistance to change) and some not (population increases, inflation) were the cause of a gradual internal decline which finally showed itself to the outside world as military failure and loss of territory.

The research of young, modern Turkish historians into the archives of the Ottoman empire is shedding new light on the nature of the Ottoman decline. Unfortunately, so far very little of this research is available in translation, but when it is, it seems certain to provide new theories to challenge traditional western views.

Making notes on 'Reasons for the Decline of the Ottoman Empire'

The previous chapter looked at the date of decline of the Ottoman empire as apparent in foreign affairs. This chapter considers the symptoms and causes of internal decline, what the Ottomans thought was wrong, and what they tried to do about it. Could they have done anything more? Making notes, using the following headings and sub-headings, may help you to answer that question:

1.   The date of decline
1.1. The Ottoman view – the Circle of Equity
2.   The Ottoman view of the reasons for decline

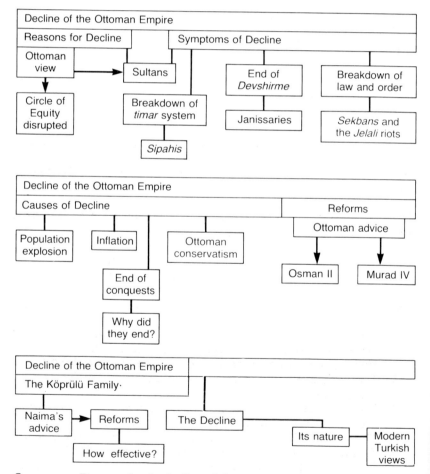

Summary – Reasons for the decline of the Ottoman Empire

Answering essay questions on 'Reasons for the Decline of the Ottoman Empire'

Questions you are likely to be asked on this topic are all disguised variations of:

A. Why did the Ottomans cease to threaten Europe?
B. When did the Ottoman cease to threaten Europe?

The trick is to recognise the variations. For example you might meet:

1. 'Account for the failure of the Ottomans to make substantial territorial gains in Europe between 1566 and 1683'.
2. 'Why did the Ottoman threat to Europe decline after 1566?'
3. 'Did difficulties within the Ottoman empire bring the Turkish threat to an end in Europe?'
4. 'To what extent was the increased efficiency of the Christian forces responsible for the end of Ottoman conquests in Europe?'
5. 'When did the Turkish menace cease to be important in Europe?'
6. 'Was the end of Ottoman expansion in Europe inevitable?'
7. 'What were the limitations on the Ottoman empire's continued expansion in Europe?'

8. '"The Ottoman threat to Europe substantially diminished during the second half of the sixteenth century." Is this view accurate?'

Which questions belong to category A and which to category B? Which question requires some discussion of both the 'Why' and the 'When' issues? Which questions require a series of 'because' answers? Which questions require a two-part 'to this extent, yes . . . to this extent, no' answer?

Source-based questions on *'Reasons for the Decline of the Ottoman Empire'*

1 The Circle of Equity
Read the extracts on page 118, and study the diagram of the Circle of Equity on page 117. Answer the following questions:
a) Explain the terms *askeri* and *reaya*.
b) Under what circumstances does the author of the first extract expect there to be a reduction in state revenue?
c) What evidence is provided by the writer of the second extract to support his contention that the old order was in decline?
d) Was the Circle of Equity an accurate representation of the political and social organisation of the Ottoman empire? Explain your answer.

CHAPTER 7

The Empire Observed

From the beginning the Ottoman empire was a source of fear and fascination to western Europe. It was an incomprehensible, strange and secret country. That it had emerged at all was regarded as a near miracle. It was on this miraculous aspect that westerners, now as then, have tended to dwell. The empire was 'a rendezvous for adventurers and fanatics – a region of unparalleled mystical enthusiasm, where war and religion marched hand in hand', and was quite unlike anything in post-medieval Europe. No wonder the west was both attracted and repelled by the accounts which ambassadors, merchants and a few intrepid travellers brought back, describing what they had seen and heard in the sixteenth and seventeenth centuries.

1 Contemporary Western Accounts

The Venetian *bailos* (representatives) stationed in Istanbul were very conscientious in reporting home, and their reports are still available in the Venetian archives. While most were content to describe, with varying degrees of approval, the palace slave system and its workings, not all Venetians were favourably impressed by what they saw. One, Matteo Zane, writing in the 1590s was scathing in his condemnation of the Ottomans:

1 The Turks are partly native and partly renegade [i.e. convert slaves]. The natives, who live for the most part in Asia, are, in comparison with the renegades, less depraved and less tyrannous, because they still have some religion in them, which the others
5 have not, the most scoundrelly men that can be imagined, having seemingly, with the true faith, lost all humanity. They have become like this by seeing placed in their hands the arms, government and riches of the whole empire.

Much of the information available to us on the sixteenth century comes from the tireless Ogier Ghiselin de Busbecq, the Austrian ambassador to Istanbul. He was a careful and meticulous observer, who made every effort to understand what he saw and to report it fairly. In the four very long letters, which together form a fair-sized book, and which he sent to his friend, the Austrian ambassador in Lisbon, he wrote endearingly of his experiences at Suleiman's court between 1554 and 1562, although they included a lengthy period of house arrest. This was at a time when Suleiman was displeased with the Emperor

Ferdinand in the matter of negotiations for a treaty. De Busbecq, alone, of the western observers of his day, treats the Ottomans as friends, and not as freaks of nature. Even the dread Janissaries, whom he met on his journey through the Balkans to Istanbul, have a touching naivety ascribed to them. He describes how two of them came to his room at the inn where he was staying, and, rushing towards him, thrust bunches of hyacinths and narcissi into his hand. 'The Turks', he observes, 'are very fond of flowers'. He goes on, 'If I had not been told that they were Janissaries, I could well have believed that they were some kind of Turkish monk, or members of some religious society; yet these are the famous Janissaries, who carry such terror wherever they go.'

Very few individuals, and particularly Englishmen, made the long trip to Istanbul in the sixteenth century. One who did was Thomas Dallam, a timorous clock-maker from London, who after a six month journey full of alarms, arrived safely in Istanbul in August 1599. He brought with him an elaborate combined clock and organ, a present from Elizabeth I to Mehmed III. The sea voyage had done nothing to improve the machinery, which had come unglued, but Dallam was able

Suleiman receiving a European visitor, probably John Sigismund Zapolya

to repair it and to present it to Mehmed. The Sultan was much impressed when the clock first struck 22, and then 16 bells, two trumpets, and a holly bush full of automated singing blackbirds burst into a four part melody, accompanied by music from the organ itself.

Dallam was rather overwhelmed by the Sultan and his attendants, who included 200 pages dressed in cloth of gold, 'with the heads shaved, apart from a lock of hair behind each ear, like squirrels' tails.' Eventually he was called upon to play the organ for the Sultan. He went forward very anxiously, worried in case he should touch the Sultan who was sitting close to the instrument 'on a chair of estate, on his thumb a ring with a diamond half an inch square, and a fair scimitar by his side.' The Sultan stood up in order to see better and accidentally pushed Dallam, who immediately assumed that his head was about to be cut off. Fortunately his fears proved groundless, and he was afterwards given a 'handful of gold' for playing so well.

Thomas Dallam is notable for being the only Westerner to give us first hand evidence about the harem at this time:

1 Crossing through the little square court paved with marble he [a black eunuch] pointed to me to go to a grating in the wall . . . the wall was very thick and grated on both sides with iron very strongly . . . but through it I did see 30 of the Grand Signor's
5 concubines – and very pretty ones indeed – that were playing with a ball in another court. The hair of their heads hung down their backs, plaited together with a tassel of small pearls hanging at the lower end. I stood so long, that he who had showed me all this
10 kindness began to be very angry with me.

The only other westerner known to have seen anything of the harem, by using a telescope to inspect the Sultan and his ladies in the garden, is said to have been hanged in 1680 at the window from which he had committed the crime.

a) How Reliable?

How far can we rely on reports like these? How many western observers understood what they saw and heard, and how much of their reports were in fact hearsay, or designed simply to amaze, to entertain, or to draw attention, by comparison, to deficiencies or excellences at home?

De Busbecq must be regarded as outstanding, for his letters are, without question, the most revealing extant description by a foreigner of the Ottoman empire at the height of its glory. De Busbecq was a remarkable individual – a diplomat, traveller, linguist, scholar, anti-quarian, zoologist and biologist, who brought back over 200 classical manuscripts to Vienna, and who introduced the lilac and the tulip into western Europe. He was fair in his comments, giving credit where it was due, and criticising where he thought it necessary, and as far as we can tell, he was an accurate reporter. He was *persona grata* at Suleiman's court, and on familiar terms with the great officials. He did not like Rustem Pasha, whom he distrusted, believing, rightly, that the Grand Vezir was corrupt. Nevertheless, they seem to have spoken together quite frequently, and much of de Busbecq's inside knowledge must have come through Rustem Pasha. Almost all the other European obervers' writings tell us more about *their* prejudices, misconceptions and ignorance than about the Ottoman empire of their day. While we cannot afford to reject their evidence out of hand, we need to be aware that by relying too heavily upon it, we are likely to distort the truth, as we should if we relied on similar material by foreign observers when writing the history of western Europe.

The problem of the reliability of western evidence about the sixteenth and seventeenth-century Ottoman empire, is one which has exercised the minds of western historians for many years. A. H. Lybyer in 1913 considered that 'the writings of these men of various western nationalities are in a way more helpful than a similar number of books by native writers, because foreigners could usually take nothing for granted, but were compelled to draw a complete picture'. But he did admit that they 'could not get at the inner springs of the Ottoman activity as well as the native could.' Lybyer's important book on government at the time of Suleiman relies very heavily on the evidence of foreigners, and recent Turkish research has shown him to have been misled in some ways as a result, particularly in his belief in the sharp division between the Ruling and the Religious Institutions. Such evidence from Ottoman sources as Lybyer needed to enable him to present a more balanced picture was not available to him.

Half a century later, the situation had changed little, when F. Braudel wrote that 'as western historians, we have seen only the outer face of the Turkish empire . . . We have been obliged to turn to historical literature, travellers' tales . . . and above all to western sources. The history of Turkey . . . has been approached from outside, deduced rather than ascertained, from random evidence of dispatches written by westerners.' Braudel is making a number of important points here. The Ottoman empire was secretive and inward looking, with little direct contact with western Europe, except in military matters. Western observers had little sympathy with a religion and culture which was so different, or with a system of government which was so alien. As a result it was inevitable that western views of the Ottomans would be superficial and incomplete.

Modern historians such as N. Itzkowitz have begun to remedy this situation. He writes of the need to 'allow the Ottomans to speak for themselves', so that 'we can penetrate beyond the surface view provided by the insights of western observers of the Ottoman world to the core of Ottoman existence'. The only way to do this is to make use of the great riches of archive material available in Turkey. Although a start on this has been made in recent years, much of the material is still unclassified and little of it is yet available in translation. But it is there, and in time will open the way to a better understanding of the Ottoman empire, seen from the inside.

In the meantime, some material is available from contemporary Ottoman writers. Most of them were historians, for, from the early sixteenth century onwards, history became an important subject of study.

2 Contemporary Ottoman Accounts

How did the Ottomans see themselves in the sixteenth and seventeenth centuries? European observers have always wrongly maintained that Ottoman strength lay in military achievement and political organisation, and had little or no cultural content. This was certainly not true of architecture and the decorative arts, nor was it true of literature. Poetry was the main literary form. Only in the writing of history was prose extensively used.

The sixteenth and seventeenth centuries saw a great interest in historical writing, perhaps as a way of emphasising that the *ghazi* state had come of age as the Ottoman empire, and was now both established and respectable, with a history behind it. Most of this historical writing was concerned with dynastic or military affairs; there is very little anecdotal or 'human interest' material to be found in it. This is because its origins lie in the tradition of the chroniclers, who were employed by government officers to keep a straightforward account of present events as they occurred, or to use earlier records to write a history of past events. In the seventeenth century an official court chronicler was appointed, whose job was to keep a 'day book' or diary of the sultan's activities. He also had access to state papers for the purpose of accurately recording government decisions and decrees. But he was not allowed to comment, evaluate or appraise the events which he recorded.

There were, however, some historians who broke out of this straightjacket. The most important of these was Mustafa Naima Efendi (1665–1716), who, although a court historian, also acted as a spokesman for the Grand Vezir Hussein Köprülü at the time of Karlowitz. He wrote about the practice of history in terms that are relevant today and, at the time, compared favourably with historical writing in western Europe. He wrote about the role of historians:

1 They must be reliable in what they say and must not make foolish statements or write spurious tales. If they do not know the truth about any particular question they should address themselves to those who have fathomed it, and only then put down what they
5 have ascertained to be the fact ... They should disregard the

disquieting rumours which are gossiped about among the common people. Instead they must prefer the reliable documented statement of men who know how to record what actually hap-
10 pened . . . Historians ought first to inform themselves, from those who have proper information concerning the question in hand, what it was that men thought and what it was they believed to be the best course in the conduct of the war and in making terms
15 with the foe, what were the causes and the weaknesses which were then bringing triumph or entailing destruction . . . Historians should speak frankly and fairly . . . they should not exaggerate . . . and if, to attain their end, they must criticise and censure
20 great men, they should never be unjust. In any case they must take care to present the real nature of the question, regardless of what it may be . . .

Naima followed his own precepts in all that he wrote. His history covered the years 1591 to 1660, as well as his own times. He analysed and explained events, using information from many different sources, such as the chronicles, and the state archives. He also made use of the writings of earlier historians, such as Katip Chelebi whose *Compendium* covered the years 1591 to 1655, and of his own experiences, as well as the reminiscences of friends and the testimony of men in high places and others in a position to know the truth. Without Naima's work our understanding of Ottoman history would be the poorer.

Evliya Chelebi (1611–1680) was one of the few Ottomans who travelled extensively, and who wrote about what he saw inside (and outside) the empire. Unfortunately, of the ten volumes which he filled with his jottings, only two have been translated into English. These deal mostly with events and places inside the empire, especially in and around Istanbul, during the 1630s.

Evliya came from a wealthy dervish family. His father, who lived to be nearly 100 had fought in Suleiman's army in 1566. His mother was a slave girl from the Caucasus. Extremely pious, Evliya was early admitted as a member of the *ulema*. At the advanced age of 25 through the influence of an uncle, he was appointed as page to Murad IV, whom he accompanied on a number of campaigns (see page 133). Two years later he joined the Sipahis of the Porte, before eventually returning to his career in the *ulema*. Between 1640 and 1668 he travelled throughout Anatolia and the Balkans, made the pilgrimage to Mecca, visited Egypt, and was present at the siege of Candia during the War of Crete. After arriving at Vienna in 1665, he received special permission from the sultan to extend his tour to cover Germany, the Netherlands, Scandinavia and Poland. He was undoubtedly the most travelled Ottoman of his day.

A most remarkable man, he was cultured, inquisitive and gullible, very gifted musically, interested in sport of all kinds, fond of gardens and flowers and a connoisseur of food. He was also conceited, self-opinionated and extremely bigoted – he hated the Jews and despised the Persians. In a typically Ottoman way he regarded any non-Moslem, or anything outside the empire as of little value. Nevertheless, he still manages to come over as a likeable person and a sympathetic observer, perhaps because his books are full of little jokes.

His greatest value to the modern historian (at least until his later books on his foreign travel are available) is the variety of information on urban society embedded in the hotchpotch of his writings. In 1630 he began a complete descriptive survey of the city of Istanbul, ward by ward, noting down its buildings and monuments, as well as the occupations, entertainments and habits of its people, what they ate and drank and what they wore. He was privileged to be present at the casting of the great bronze cannon, not seen by any except the privileged, for the presence of 'any with evil eyes' would have caused the metal to fail. In 1638 he saw and described in great detail the three-day procession of 735 trade guilds through the streets of the capital. He writes graphically of such exotic Companies as the Executioners, carrying the gruesome tools of their trade, the Lion-keepers, with lumps of meat seasoned with opium to calm their frenzied charges, the Slave-dealers, with their wares attractively decked out, the Storytellers, so old they had to be carried in litters, and the Fireworkmakers, letting off samples of their work among the spectators. He is equally concerned with the more ordinary tradespeople, the bakers, the butchers, the fruiterers and so on.

Discounting his tendency to exaggerate, his insistence on tracing the origins of all customs back to the Prophet, and his love of the marvellous and mythical, Evliya is invaluable as a seventeenth-century source. He is at his best when writing about the urban society which he knew best, providing us with information which is not available anywhere else.

a) How Complete?

Our knowledge of day-to-day life within the Ottoman empire as a whole is, however, very limited, substantially more so than in most of the countries of western Europe in the period 1450 to 1700. Most of what we know concerns the lives of those in high places, the sultans, the important officials, the army, and the *ulema*, and the events which touched their lives: battles, treaties, the court and the economy. We know almost nothing about the peasants, the *reaya*. The cadastral (tax) registers are their only record, and, given the nature of Ottoman society, are likely to remain so. As long as the peasants worked the land in comparative contentment and paid their taxes, they were of no concern as individuals. We know little more about the townspeople as individuals, the merchants, craftsmen and artisans who traded or made the goods that are listed and described in treasury inventories, guild records, fixed price registers and market regulations. But because their social and economic status was higher than that of the *reaya*, it seems possible that future research among the state archives may shed some light on the social history of at least some of these citizens. Within the *askeri* class, recent investigations by Turkish historians are beginning to provide personal details, for instance, about some *timar* holders and their attempts to evade military service by feigning illness. Ottoman records are essentially matter of fact, and non-anecdotal, for in an absolutist state the individual is unimportant, except in relation to the welfare of that state. Nevertheless, recent research in Turkish archives has already enabled the writing of Ottoman social history to begin, particularly for the seventeenth century. There is every hope, therefore, that our present very partial knowledge of life within the empire will soon be greatly extended.

Making notes on 'The Empire Observed'

Both western and Ottoman contemporary views of the empire are presented here. The important question at issue is how reliable is such evidence for our understanding of the empire. Use the following headings and sub-headings to make notes on this short chapter:
1.   Contemporary western views
1.1. How reliable?
2.   Contemporary Ottoman views
2.1. How complete?

Source-based questions on 'The Empire Observed'

1 Mustafa Naima Efendi, the Historian (1665–1716)
Read the extract from Naima's writings on pages 147–8. Answer the following questions:
a) What assumptions does Naima make about historical truth?
b) Which of Naima's precepts were in conflict with the prevailing expectations of the seventeenth-century Ottoman empire? Explain your answer.
c) Which of Naima's precepts are valid for modern-day historical writing? Which are not? Explain your answer.

CHAPTER 8

The Impact of the Ottoman Empire on Europe

1 'The Great Fear'

Between 1480 and 1609, 80 books were published in France alone on the Ottoman Empire. Some of these books were serious and scholarly works, but the great majority were crude anti-Turkish propaganda. So great an impression had the 'Turkish menace' made on the countries of western Europe, that everywhere the Turks were portrayed as objects of hatred and horror. Especially in central Europe, they produced the 'Great Fear' among educated and uneducated, rich and poor alike.

Part of the enmity had a religious basis. Luther played on this in his War Sermon of 1529, in which he presented the Turks as fulfilling the prophecy of Ezekiel, 'Satan will be loosed from his prison', and that of Revelations, 'I will bring the worst of the nations to take possession of their houses.' Another Protestant preacher was thundering a century later, 'We must not be amazed if God is now punishing the Christians through the Turks – for they are the rod and scourge and fury of God.'

In the popular mind the Turks were barbarous, uncivilised and violent. One of the best sellers of the sixteenth century was *The Miseries and Tribulations of the Christians held in Tribute and Slavery by the Turks*, originally published in the Balkans. Illustrated with lurid woodcuts showing imaginary scenes of Turkish cruelty and torture, it ran into many editions. It was vastly popular and did much to reinforce Christian prejudices against 'those worse than dogs, in all their works'.

Shortly after the fall of Constantinople, even a man as educated as the Greek theologian and Platonist scholar, Cardinal Bessarion, was writing intemperately to the Doge of Venice of 'the most inhuman barbarians, the fiercest of wild beasts and the most ferocious animals who now threatened danger to Italy with their violent assaults.' The Cardinal himself would probably have seen his public denunciation of the Moslem hordes as simply a continuation into modern times of what medieval writers had called the 'World's Debate', the conflict between Islam and the 'common corps of Christendom'.

But by the middle of the fifteenth century, the common corps of Christendom was already *in extremis*. Pope Pius II decribed it as 'a body without a head, a republic without laws or magistrates . . . every state has a separate prince, and every prince has a separate interest. Who will make the English love the French? Who will unite the Genoese and the Aragonese? Who will reconcile the Germans with the Hungarians and the Bohemians? If you lead a small army against the Turks, you will easily be overcome; if a large one, it will soon fall'.

However, even as the concept of Christendom was losing its meaning, splintered by the Reformation, and by the growth of new ideas of national identity, it was still possible as late as the 1590s, for volunteers, both Catholic and Protestant, to combine forces unofficially in the defence of Austria against the Turks. These volunteers came from all over Europe to take part in what they described as a crusade, a fight for hearth and home and Christianity. Perhaps this was because the feeling remained in Europe that the Ottoman empire was 'different', not just in religion, but in some indefinable way, from other states. When James I of England described war against the Turks as 'a battle in the public cause', he was only following established tradition. An Elizabethan jurist had managed to make out a case that, while all war against fellow human beings was wrong, war against the Turks was 'almost natural', and 'because of their insatiable aggressiveness, we constantly have a legitimate reason for war.'

A sober observer like de Busbecq, usually so restrained in his language, could write in passionate style of the horrors to be expected from Suleiman's next campaign:

1 The sultan stands before us with all the terror inspired by his own
   successes and those of his ancestors; he over runs the plains of
   Hungary with 200000 horsemen; he threatens Austria; he
   menaces the rest of Germany; he brings in his train all the nations
5 between here and the Persian frontier. He is at the head of an
   army equipped with the resources of many kingdoms . . . Like a
   thunderbolt, he smites, shatters and destroys whatever stands in
   his way; he is at the head of veteran troops, and a highly trained
10 army which is accustomed to leadership; he spreads far and wide
   the terror of his name. He roars like a lion along our frontier,
   seeking to break through, now here, now there.

Half a century later, Richard Knolles in his *History of the Turks*, still thought of the Turkish army as the greatest terror of the world. This traditional idea that the Ottoman Turks were a barbarian horde, which carried with it rapine, destruction and terror wherever it went, is deeply rooted in European consciousness. But it is wrong. The Ottoman army was not a barbarian horde. It was highly disciplined and well led. However, as it moved west through the Balkans it was preceded by fast irregular cavalry units, *akinjis*, who travelled far ahead of the main army. They served the sultan, not for pay but for what plunder they could get, and they made sure that they got it. These outriders were the soldiers with whom most of the Balkan people came into contact, and it is not surprising that these marauding horsemen came to represent the Ottoman army in the popular mind.

2 Influence of the Ottomans on the Balkans

As de Busbecq wrote,

1 It was the capture of Belgrade (August 1521) which threw open
the floodgates through which the barbarians entered to devastate
Hungary. It brought about the death of King Louis, the loss of
Buda and the enslavement of Transylvania. If the Turks had not
5 captured Belgrade they would not have entered Hungary, once
one of the most flourishing kingdoms of Europe, and now a
desolate and ravaged land.

The capture of Belgrade, the battle of Mohaçs (1526) and the siege of
Vienna (1529) laid waste great areas of Hungary, so that a century and a
half later, when the Ottoman army again advanced on Vienna, the
evidence of Suleiman's ravages were still clearly visible. The countryside was economically backward, sparsely populated, agriculturally
primitive and poor. How far were the Ottomans responsible for the
condition of the Balkans at the end of the seventeenth century?
    The Ottomans took over the former Byzantine lands of the Balkans
and their rule there continued for 500 years, from the Danube in the
north to the borders of Italy and the Dalmatian coast in the west,
through Croatia and Serbia to Greece in the south – an immense, largely
mountainous expanse of land covering about 750000 square miles.
    Even now very little detailed information is available about the
Ottomans in south-east Europe. Until recently Balkan historians
tended either to treat this period of their history in a biased, angry and
emotive way or, more often, to ignore it completely. Only since the
1950s have they begun to make use of their archives. Now, as P. F.
Sugar points out, while 'the Ottomans are still considered to have
brought mainly disaster to the people of south-east Europe, this
evaluation is now based on the study of records and not ascribed to the
planned inhuman, wilfully destructive behaviour of barbaric Asiatic
hordes.'
    The traditional European view has been to blame the Ottoman
occupation for the 'backwardness' of the Balkans and to leave it at that.
But this view must be open to question, for there is no evidence that
any non-Moslem lands in south-east Europe were any more 'advanced'
politically, socially or economically than those under Ottoman control,
at least until the late nineteenth century. The traditional European view
has also been that of the Balkan Christians languishing under the heel of
the bloodthirsty Turkish conquerors. This idea, based mainly on
Papal/Habsburg propaganda, is now largely discredited. There is,
however, a real danger that historians may be moving too far in the
other direction, and presenting the Ottomans as the benevolent liber-
ators of the Balkan peoples. The truth lies between the two extremes.

Although the Ottomans took lands, plunder and slaves by force, it was to their advantage to protect the peasants, who worked the land and paid the taxes to support the *sipahi* army. Not until the later seventeenth century, as central control weakened, abuses crept into the provincial administration and inflation took its toll, did the peasants suffer from high taxation, oppression and injustice. It was not the original conquest, but the long and bitter wars and the guerilla fighting which followed, which destroyed the land and with it the peasants' livelihood, so that in some areas they were forced to revert from arable farming to a semi-nomadic pastoral existence over a period of several generations.

The greatest effect of the Ottoman conquest of the Balkans was felt initially by the aristocracy. Ottoman society was a meritocracy, without any hereditary nobility, quite unlike any European state of the time. The Balkan nobility could not be fitted into the Ottoman scheme of things, and presented in any case a potential danger as a focus of revolt. The majority needed, therefore, to be eliminated, and this was speedily done. There were some whose lives were spared for various reasons. They were absorbed into the Ottoman ruling class, after conversion to Islam, and most of them were granted *timars*.

Other changes were brought about in the Balkans as a result of Ottoman policies. Profound changes in the social and religious balance of the region resulted from the wholesale resettlement of the native Christian population in new areas, and the settlement of Moslem peasants, forced to emigrate from Anatolia, in sparsely populated areas of the Balkans. This led to a complete confusion of national identities, unimportant to the Ottomans whose political organisation took no account of differing nationalities within the empire (it was a man's occupation and religion, not ethnic origins which counted). The immigration of large numbers of Moslems into a previously Christian region, does not seem to have caused any serious problems, largely because each religious community kept itself to itself. The loss of young men and boys from Christian areas, through the operation of the *devshirme* system, and the reorganisation of the land into *timars* altered the whole pattern of life in the Balkans. It does not, however, seem to have been any worse for the peasants, whose life under the native Balkan nobility had been harsh. It may even, at least in the sixteenth century, have been better. Under the Ottomans, taxation was fairer, the old feudal labour services had been remitted, and law and order was better maintained.

Although the Ottoman socio-economic structure in the Balkans was very strictly controlled, it was also surprisingly lenient. Some western historians have always believed that the state had little interest in the people, as long as they remained obedient, and performed their military or agricultural obligations. This idea has been recently challenged. The numerous edicts issued by the sultan to prevent possible oppression of the *reaya* and the non-Moslem *zimmis* are cited by Turkish historians as evidence of Ottoman concern for the peasants of the Balkans. The government's motives may have been altruistic, although it seems more probable that they were financial; after all, the peasants, through their work on the land and their payment of taxes, were the basis of the Ottoman economy. It was important, therefore, to protect them so that they could fulfil their economic function in society. Independent political, and to some extent, cultural life came to an end for the Balkan Christians, although they were allowed a degree of freedom to organise themselves in small local communities under their own elected leaders, subject of course to Ottoman provincial administration.

The Ottomans were religiously tolerant of their Balkan subjects, and there was no pressure to convert to Islam. However, mixed marriages were common between Moslem men and Christian women. This was partly because with this type of inter-faith marriage the father of the bride did not have to provide a dowry, as he would if his daughter married a Christian, and he also received the customary Moslem bride-price from the groom. Financially, it was extremely advantageous to the girl's family, and there were no religious objections by the Church, for she was allowed to remain Christian after her marriage. Her daughters would be allowed to remain Christians, and her sons as Moslems, thus exempting them from the *devshirme*. Because Moslems paid only land tax, while Christians paid a poll tax as well, there were financial advantages in conversion, but no other pressure was applied, apart from energetic missionary work by itinerant Moslem groups like the dervishes. Only in a few areas of the Balkans was there large scale 'turkification', as conversion was called, and that was usually close to places where the Anatolian peasants had been resettled. In most areas the Christians, while not being absorbed into the Moslem society, accepted that it was there, accommodated it, and continued their own way of life as before.

One area of the Balkans was exceptional in the degree of autonomy it retained. This was the tiny republic of Ragusa (Dubrovnik) on the Dalmatian coast. It was an Italian merchant commune, hemmed in on the landward side by Ottoman controlled Bosnia and Herzogovina, and only retaining its independence by payment of a substantial annual cash tribute, and by virtue of its commercial usefulness to the Ottoman empire. Ragusa organised the salt trade, dealt in textiles and gold and silver, and later in the sixteenth century became the chief supplier of firearms and ammunition for the area. By the end of the 1580s as Genoa and Venice lost importance under Ottoman pressure, Ragusa took over much of their carrying trade, with a large fleet of 'great ships' worked by over 5000 seamen. It was a point of contact between east and west, and a meeting place for spies and secret agents from both sides, reporting on enemy intentions. It grew rich on the pickings.

One other result of the Ottoman conquest of the Balkans was the construction by their Christian neighbours of a chain of defensive fortresses, a sort of early 'Iron Curtain', separating the two civilisations. The Ottomans built no such defensive lines until the later part of the seventeenth century. When they did so, it was an acknowledgement that they had reached the limits of their expansion.

3 Conflict with Venice

The Republic of Venice, like its rival Genoa, had acquired trading bases and commercial privileges, known as 'capitulations', within the Byzantine empire during the fourteenth and fifteenth centuries. The situation continued, and additional bases, notably the island of Cyprus in 1489, were obtained by diplomacy or conquest after Ottoman expansion into the Balkans and the eastern Mediterranean. From these bases the Venetians traded dried fruit, spices, silks, alum, oil, wine and grain from the Middle East in exchange for European wool and woollen cloth. Commercial privileges giving trading rights in Istanbul and elsewhere in the empire were normally granted in return for an annual payment, but were sometimes paid for by the provision of information useful to the Ottomans, for example on the activities of Charles V in 1533. But these privileges could be, and often were, withdrawn at short notice; the Ottomans used them as a political weapon. The Venetian capitulation to trade in wheat was dependent not only on payment of duty, but on an agreement to remain at peace with the empire. Any aggressive movement by Venice led to a withdrawal of the capitulations. In the war of 1463–79 the Ottomans not only withdrew the capitulations, but actively encouraged Florence and Ragusa to take over from Venice. At the end of the war the status quo was resumed. This became the pattern of Ottoman–Venetian relations.

Until 1569 Venice remained the main sea power in the area, for before that neither the Ottomans nor any other state in the region was strong enough to change the situation. Up to the end of the sixteenth century Venice handled most of the Ottoman trade with the west, in the intervals between a series of wars between the two countries, culminating in the Ottoman attack on Cyprus. The seventeenth century saw the armed conflict continuing, with the Venetian loss of Crete and the Ottoman humiliation of the Treaty of Karlowitz.

Although the Portuguese discovery and exploitation of the Cape route to the spice centres of India and the Far East had caused trading difficulties for the Venetians in the eastern Mediterranean in the early sixteenth century, the problems were overcome. By 1560 there was as much pepper being bought and sold in Alexandria as there was in Lisbon, and in the following year accounts show that the German spice merchants in Venice were paying more than double the taxes they had paid in 1490 (i.e. before the discovery of the Cape route). Throughout the 1560s the Venetian economy was booming. Shipbuilding, ceramics, sugar refining, printing and glass working were all thriving industries quite apart from the valuable import/export and carrying trades. The population had increased by 50% since the early years of the century and all seemed well. But the protracted naval wars with the Ottoman empire for domination of the eastern Mediterranean, and the need to fortify her overseas trading bases and her Balkan land frontiers were placing a great strain on Venetian resources. The loss of Cyprus in 1570 was a bitter blow both to her prestige and to her economic prosperity, for the island was not only an important grain and wine producing centre, but was also a port of call for Venetian galleys trading with Egypt and Syria, and with Anatolia.

By the early seventeenth century the Venetian economy was in recession. In particular, the export trade in woollen textiles had declined sharply. Instead of 25 000 lengths of cloth a year being sent to Istanbul as had been the case at the end of the sixteenth century, in 1611 there were less than half that number, with the expectation of further reductions in the next few years. The scale of this economic recession is supported by Venetian state documents which place the initial blame on the disastrous war over Cyprus (1570–73). There were other factors involved in the recession, including the excessive and stifling control over industry exercised by the Venetian government, and the great increase in the cost of marine insurance brought about by continuing war in the Mediterranean which made the carrying trade much less profitable. After 1600 English and Dutch sailing ships, faster and bigger than the Venetian galleys, appeared in the Mediterranean, carrying cheap cloth and the tin needed for casting the new bronze cannon. The number of corsairs, both Moslem and Christian increased yearly, causing great loss and damage to shipping generally, while the depradations of the Serbs and Bosnians settled by the Habsburgs in Cariniola led Venice into another expensive war. The long drawn out conflict with the Ottomans, lasting 22 years, and ending with the loss of the important island colony of Crete in 1669, left Venetian influence in the Mediterranean much reduced.

The numerous wars between the Ottomans and Venice (1423–30, 1463–79, 1499–1502, 1570–73, 1645–69, 1684–95), Ottoman expansion in the Balkans, the increase of Ottoman naval power in the Mediterranean, and Ottoman encouragement for Florence and Ragusa in their trade rivalry with Venice, all contributed to Venetian political and economic decline. While they were not the only cause, the activities of the Ottomans played a considerable part in the downfall of Venice during the sixteenth and seventeenth centuries.

4 Breakout to the West

A recent comment that European historians traditionally treat the Ottomans as 'noises off' is only too true. They are allowed to come on stage for a brief time, only to be 'decisively defeated' at Lepanto, after which they conveniently 'decline' into speedy oblivion. Their sole contribution of any importance to the mainstream of European history is said to be their restriction of oriental trade, particularly the spice trade through the Levant, leading therefore to a European maritime 'breakout to the west'.

Chronologically, this is a very suspect theory. The Portuguese had circumnavigated Africa and had established a chain of trading stations across the Far East and the Indian Ocean before Selim I seized the ports of Egypt and Syria. In other words, the Portuguese had reached the Red Sea, India and beyond *before* the Ottomans had placed any new geographical or political obstacles in the way of the spice trade through the eastern Mediterranean.

There is evidence that the Portuguese planned from the beginning to eliminate the Moslem interest in the spice trade – 'Mohammed will be destroyed, and destroyed he cannot help but be.' Ottoman military activity after 1515 can be interpreted as a reply to this western policy. Selim's invasion of Syria and Egypt in 1516–17 gave them control over Alexandria and Beirut, the major spice ports. The attack on Rhodes and its capture was essential to protect the sea lanes between these ports and Istanbul. Some Turkish historians would go further. They see Selim's drive into the Hejaz and towards the Red Sea as a direct response to Vasco da Gama's circumnavigation of Africa and the resulting Portuguese presence in the Indian Ocean.

It is true to say that western Europe was expanding economically at this time, and when the Ottomans effectively blocked off the exits from the eastern Mediterranean new trade outlets were needed and found. But it is not true to say that a 'breakout to the west' was precipitated by Ottoman action in Egypt and Syria. The breakout had already occurred before the Ottoman expansion. The New World had already been discovered, Africa had already been circumnavigated, and sea routes to the Far East had been established. The driving force of western exploration was not, as western historians are fond of writing, because 'the Moslem empire now stood between east and west, and European traders were determined to find a sea route to the orient'. The reasons were quite other, and lay in the economic, technical and intellectual developments of Renaissance Europe.

5 European Politics

Ottoman relations with the Habsburgs were always fraught with tension. In the sixteenth century the areas of conflict with the Spanish Habsburgs centred on North Africa, and with the Austrian Habsburgs on the Balkan frontier and the disputed area of Hungary. In both cases the disputes were intensified by religious differences. In North Africa the Ottomans used both military and naval means to support their fellow Moslems there against the Catholic king of Spain, in Tripoli and Tunis, and through the activities of the corsairs. In the Balkans by providing a military threat to the frontiers of the Holy Roman Empire, the Moslem Ottomans enabled the Lutheran Protestants to wring concessions from the Catholic Emperor. From 1526 onwards, all major concessions were the direct result of Ottoman activities in eastern and central Europe. Suleiman, encouraged by the French, wrote to the German princes of the Schmalkaldic League suggesting the need for co-operation against Charles V and the Pope. He pointed out what he regarded as similarities between Protestants and Moslems, based on their abhorrence of idols. It is arguable that Ottoman imperialism was the largest single factor in the consolidation and legitimation of Lutheranism. In Hungary under Ottoman protection, Calvinism spread so widely it came to be called the country of Calvinoturcismus. To support Lutherans and Calvinists against Catholic Habsburgs became an essential part of Ottoman foreign policy. By this means they encouraged European divisions, weakened the Habsburgs and prevented the possibility of a united crusade by the Christian powers.

In pursuit of their anti-Habsburg policy, the Ottomans were drawn into an alliance with France. For a while Europe marvelled at the sight of the Catholic King of France making the port of Toulon available to the ships of the Moslem Sultan. This French alliance came to be the cornerstone of sixteenth-century Ottoman policy in Europe. Its intention was disruptive. It was designed merely to foment Habsburg–Valois rivalry.

In the seventeenth century Ottoman influence on European politics was much less, partly because of domestic difficulties within the empire and partly because of the changed situation in Europe, where the balance of power had shifted in favour of France, and where the attention of the Austrian Habsburgs was diverted away from the Balkan frontier by the Thirty Years War. The Ottoman age of expansion was over, and its aggressive foreign policy with it. Old enemies such as Venice had declined in importance, while new enemies such as Russia were only just appearing on the political scene, and did not as yet present any serious danger.

The final, and perhaps the greatest Ottoman impact on Europe came at the very end of the seventeenth century, with the European realisation that the limits of Ottoman expansion had been reached, and that the frontiers were already receding. Receding, too, was the 'Great Fear', which had been part of the European consciousness for more than two and a half centuries. Never again would the Ottoman army present a serious threat to Europe. It had been proved to be no longer invincible. Ottoman greatness was soon to become only a myth.

6 The Impact of Europe on the Ottoman Empire

The great majority of Ottomans had no first hand knowledge of Europe. Very few had ever travelled in Europe, and the few who did, went only on official business. Europe had some, largely unreliable information about the Middle East, based on travellers' tales, but the Ottomans had almost none about Europe. The delay in introducing printing into the Ottoman empire (printed books were not available until the middle of the eighteenth century) did not help in the dissemination of information about the outside world. But even if books of travels had been available, it is unlikely that the Ottoman ruling class would have been interested in reading them. They knew very little about Europe, and were not concerned to know more. It was enough to know that Europe was inferior in every way to their own society, which was, as the *ulema* taught:

1 different from any other; it is the chosen, the holy people to
   whom is entrusted the furtherance of good, and the repression of
   evil; it is the only seat of justice and faith upon earth, the sole
   witness for God among the nations, just as the Prophet had been
5 God's witness among the Arab people.

A few Ottomans did travel, even if not very far, and Evilya Chelebi, who died in 1680, was one of them. He wrote a ten volume travel epic, mostly about parts of the empire, but he did venture outside the frontiers, on one occasion as far as western Europe (see page 148). In the 1650s Katip Chelebi, the historian, was one of the first Ottomans to be conscious of the importance of Europe. Writing his book on geography, *View of the World*, he decided that the only available Moslem sources were not adequate for Christian Europe. So he consulted a French renegade priest who had been converted to Islam. Even this limited source of rather inaccurate information put Katip Chelebi a long way ahead of his fellow Ottomans. He pleaded with the government that:

1 for the man who is in charge of affairs of state, the science of
   geography is one of the matters of which knowledge is necessary.
   If he is not familiar with what the entire earth's sphere is like, he
   should at least know the map of the Ottoman domains and that of
5 the states adjoining it . . . so that the invasion of the enemy's land
   and the defence of the frontiers becomes an easier task . . . Most
   locals are unable to sketch the map of their own home region.
   Sufficient and compelling proof of the necessity for learning this
10 science is the fact that the unbelievers by their application to and
   their esteem for this branch of learning have overrun the ports of
   India and the East Indies. Even such a miserable lot as the
   Venetians, a people whose ruler has only the rank of duke among

15 the unbeliever kings, has actually advanced to the Dardenelles of
the Ottoman domains and has set itself to oppose the all glorious
state which rules over east and west.

His pleas fell on deaf ears. The Sultan and his officers continued to
gather information on the European political scene as they always had,
but paid little attention to the new scientific, technological, economic or
intellectual developments.

The Ottomans looked back to the Golden Age of Suleiman the
Magnificent, and beyond him to Mehmed the Conqueror, and tried to
restore the empire to its condition then. They paid no attention to
changes beyond their frontiers, nor considered any possibility of change
within them. Islamic society was essentially traditional. 'Islam abhors
innovation' was the phrase drawn from the teachings of Mohammed.
'The worst things are those that are novelties, every novelty is an
innovation, every innovation is an error, and every error leads to
hell-fire', is a saying traceable to the Prophet himself.

Islam had been the driving force of the young Ottoman state, the
mainspring of the *Jihad* and the *ghazi* raid, as the *sheriat* had been the
basis of its later organisation. It is ironical that it was also its downfall,
stifling experiment and change, and leaving the Ottomans still in the
middle of the sixteenth century, while their European neighbours
moved on in time.

The Ottoman Empire remained what it had always been, inward
looking and self-satisfied. This attitude was all very well as long as the
Ottoman army and navy continued victorious; but as the west overtook
them in weaponry, military skill and ship design Ottoman defeats
became commonplace. The Ottomans increasingly lost touch with
developments around them. They had little personal contact with
Europeans. The Minister for Foreign Affairs (the *Reisulkuttab*) was one
of the very few Ottomans who met foreigners, ambassadors and
emissaries of various kinds, but he relied on interpreters drawn from
Greek families in Istanbul to conduct the purely formal interviews. It
was not until the 1790s that the Ottoman empire established any
permanent diplomatic relations with European powers. Previously
envoys were sent abroad only on temporary missions, to announce the
death of a sultan for instance, or to exchange treaties. Not until the
1820s did Ottoman officials begin to learn any foreign languages. The
Ottomans remained unaware of, and uninterested in any intellectual,
scientific or technological developments outside the empire. They were
essentially provincial in outlook, without curiosity about the world
beyond their frontiers. Although an energetic sultan in the late
eighteenth century introduced a programme of reform, known as the
New Order, it was not enough. The empire continued in its lethargy,
from which fresh applications of the medicine, of the kind prescribed
by Naima, could not rouse it. The medical analogy, traditionally used

by the Ottomans to diagnose the ills of the state, makes it appropriate that the empire should end its days in the twentieth century as 'the sick man of Europe'.

Making notes on 'The Impact of the Ottoman Empire on Europe'

Recent Turkish historical research has challenged many of the traditional western beliefs about the Ottoman empire. Make sure you are aware of these new theories, and understand their importance. The following headings should help you:
1. 'The Great Fear'
2. The Balkans
3. Venice
4. 'Breakout to the west'
5. European politics
6. The impact of Europe on the Ottoman empire

Source-based questions on 'The Impact of the Ottoman Empire on Europe'

1 Ottoman knowledge of Geography in the mid-Seventeenth Century
Read the extract from the writings of Katip Chelebi on page 160. Answer the following questions:
a) What does Katip Chelebi believe is the minimum geographical knowledge needed by government officials? What justification does he give for this contention?
b) What general arguments does Chelebi advance to support his plea for more attention to be paid to 'this branch of learning'?
c) What case can be made that a lack of geographical knowledge damaged Ottoman interests? Explain your answer.
d) Does the lack of interest in geography described by Chelebi confirm or contradict your understanding of Ottoman attitudes in the seventeenth century? Explain your answer.

OTTOMAN EMPIRE   EUROPE

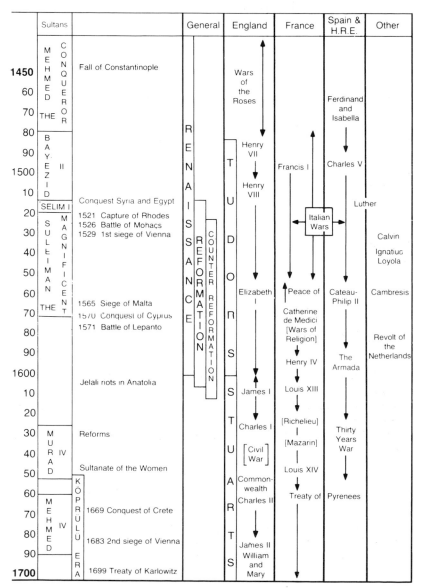

This is not a detailed or complete time chart, but a means of showing the relationship between important events and personalities in the Ottoman Empire and Europe.

Note: Suleiman the Magnificent is the almost exact contemporary of Henry VIII, Francis I and Charles V. There is no single Ottoman Sultan comparable with Elizabeth I, Catherine de Medici and Philip II.

Time Chart of the Ottoman Empire and Europe, 1450–1700

Further Reading

There are not a great many books in English on the Ottoman empire which are easily available and easily read.

Raphaela Lewis, *Everyday Life in Ottoman Turkey* (Batsford/Putnam, 1971) is a good starting point. Readable and straightforward, it is well illustrated, but is short on dates.

For some 'easy reading' try:

Anthony Bridges, *Suleiman the Magnificent* (Granada, 1983). This is entertainingly written, but with only one paragraph on Suleiman as Law giver.
Steven Runciman, *The Fall of Constantinople* (Oxford, 1961). This is the definitive account of the city's last days.
F. Babinger, *Mehmed the Conqueror and his Times* (Princeton, 1971). This often presents theory as fact and needs to be used with caution.
E. Bradford, *The Great Siege of Malta, 1565* (Penguin, 1964). This tells an exciting tale in a rousing manner.

Until recently few books by Turkish historians were available in English. One book recommended as outstanding is:

Halil Inalcik, *The Ottoman Empire, 1300 to 1600* (Weidenfeld and Nicolson, 1973).

Other useful books worth consulting are:

Norman Itzkowitz, *The Ottoman Empire and the High Islamic Tradition* (University of Chicago, 1972).
A. H. Lybyer, *Government in the Ottoman Empire in the Time of Suleiman the Magnificent* (Harvard, 1913, reprinted 1978). This is strongly European in outlook. A seminal work in its time, it is now rather out of date.
M. A. Cooke (ed.), *A History of the Ottoman Empire to 1730* (Cambridge, 1976). This is a collection of chapters from the Cambridge Modern History and the Cambridge History of Islam. Packed with facts, this volume provides a straightforward chronological account with the emphasis firmly on political history. It is short on analysis and takes little cognisance of recent Turkish research.
D. Vaughan, *Europe and the Turk* (Liverpool, 1974). This is a closely argued factual look at some of the relationships between Europe and the Ottomans. Not easy reading.

P. F. Sugar, *S.E. Europe under Ottoman Rule* (Washington, 1977). The best account of the Ottomans in the Balkans.

The only modern comprehensive history of the Ottoman empire is:

S. J. and **E. K. Shaw,** *History of the Ottoman Empire* (Cambridge, 1976) in two volumes. Volume One covers the period to 1808. It contains a number of inaccuracies and should be used with care, but its Ottoman-orientated approach is refreshing.

For its magnificent colour plates and for its scholarly insight into the cultural background of the Ottoman empire in the sixteenth century, unreservedly recommended is:

J. M. Rogers and **R. M. Ward** (eds), *Suleiman the Magnificent* (British Museum, 1988). This is the splendid catalogue for the exhibition of the same name at the British Museum in 1988.

Sources on the Ottoman Empire 1450–1700

The most importance western source is:

E. Forster (ed), *Turkish Letters of Ogier Ghiselin de Busbecq* (Oxford, 1927). In these four long letters de Busbecq provides a most perceptive and entertaining view of the empire in the sixteenth century as seen through European eyes.

It is worth trying to find a copy of:

A. Pallis, *In the Days of the Janissaries* (Hutchinson, 1951) based on the writings of Evliya Chelebi.

Glossary

These are the terms most commonly used in the text.

Aga	chief official of department of royal palace, e.g. commander of the Janissaries, chief eunuch of the harem.
akinjis	light irregular horsemen, fighting for loot not pay.
bey	an independent ruler in the early Ottoman empire – later the governor of a *sanjak*.
beylerbey	*bey* of *beys* – governor of a province made up of *sanjaks*.
cadi	judge, member of the *ulema*.
devshirme	young Christian boys collected as tribute from conquered countries in the Balkans, and trained for the sultan's service in the palace, army or administration as slaves.
divan	imperial council and court of law – originally presided over by the sultan in person, later by the Grand Vezir.
emir	prince, chief, ruling over an *emirate*.
ghazi	'warrior for the faith', whose sacred duty was to extend Islamic territory (*dar-ul-islam*=abode of Islam) and if necessary to die for it a martyr's death. Operated by making a raid (*ghaza*) into non-Moslem territory (*dar-ul-harb*=abode of war).
harem	women of the sultan's household. They lived in the *haremlik*, the women's quarters.
janissary	sultan's standing army of infantry, recruited from the *devshirme* until the mid-seventeenth century.
jelalis	bands of brigands in Anatolia around 1600.
kafes	specially guarded apartments (the cage) where royal princes were kept prisoner in the palace.
kanun	secular (sultanic) law – regulations and decrees issued by the sultan on his own authority, although they had to conform to religious (*sheriat*) law.
kul	slave (of the sultan or an important official), normally recruited from the *devshirme* or from prisoners of war or the slave markets of Istanbul.
memalik-i-mahrusa	'the well protected (by God) domains (of the sultan) – the Ottoman name for the empire.

millet	legally recognised religious community or sect, e.g. Greek Orthodox, Jew.
pasha	lord (title for a senior official).
reaya	non-military, tax-paying subjects of the sultan, usually peasants.
sanjak	the main territorial administrative unit.
sekban	an irregular soldier, equipped with firearms.
sipahi	cavalryman – either the holder of a *timar*, or a member of the sultan's slave army as a *sipahi* of the *Porte* (the palace).
sheriat	sacred Islamic law, of extreme importance in the Ottoman way of life.
shi'a	fundamentalist, heretical Moslem practice and belief – a minority within Islam.
shi'ite	follower of *shia*. The Persians were *shi'ites*.
sunnah	orthodox Moslem practice and belief – the majority within Islam.
sunnite	follower of *sunnah*. The Ottomans were *sunnites*.
timar	grant of revenues from a specified area of land (not a grant of the land itself). Used to support one or more *sipahis* for the sultan's service.
ulema	the Islamic hierarchy. Learned Moslems who provided teachers, judges and lawyers.
vakif	land and its revenues given in perpetuity as a charitable endowment for use by religious authorities.
valide	mother of a reigning sultan – sometimes the most important person in the empire.
vezir	important government official. The Grand Vezir was the chief minister.
zimmis	non-Moslem members of the *reaya* – financially disadvantaged by additional taxes.

Ottoman Titles of Respect

Aga	chief officer or official (literally 'elder brother').
Bey (Beg)	prince, later governor of district.
Cadi (Kadi)	judge, administering both *sheriat* and *kanuni* law
Chelebi	gentleman, 'Man of the Pen' (Bureaucrat, scribe), son of a reigning sultan.
Efendi	gentleman (of rather higher status than *Chelebi*).
Emir	prince.
Molla	senior member of *Ulema*.
Padishah	sultan, emperor, king of kings.
Pasha	chief officer (in government, army or navy).
Shah	emperor.

Sultan   the Ottoman ruler from fifteenth century onwards; his sons in his lifetime.

Pronunciation and Spelling

ç=ch or j
ş=sh
g is not pronounced and usually lengthens vowel, e.g. beg=bēy, aga=ā,
g before h (e.g. ghaza) and k before h (e.g. khan) are gutteral.
h in the middle of a word is a hard 'ch' (as in loch) (e.g. Mehmed).
The simplest possible forms of names and other words have been used,
and the spelling has been phoneticised as far as possible. You should
look out for spelling variations which you may meet in other books e.g.
Devşirme, devshirme; Mehmet, Mehmed; Mohammed, Muhammed;
Khaireddin, Khair-el-din, Hayruddin (Barbarossa); Suleiman, Soly-
man, Suleyman, Sulaiman; Paşa, pasha; şah, shah; so also şeria(t),
şerif, şeyh (sheikh); reaya, rayas; vakif, wakf, waqf; valide, walide;
sajak, sandjak, sanjaq, sançak; kanun, quanun; kadi, cadi, quadis;
vezir, wazir, vizier.
Note: Constantinople is referred to throughout the book as Istanbul
after its capture in 1453.

Acknowledgements

The publishers would like to thank the following for their permission to
reproduce copyright illustrations:

Reproduced by courtesy of the British Museum, cover and page 55;
National Maritime Museum, London, page 101; Topkapi Saray
Museum, Istanbul, pages 36, 68, 144.

Index